William Ernest Henley

Memorial Catalogue of the French and Dutch Loan Collection

William Ernest Henley

Memorial Catalogue of the French and Dutch Loan Collection

ISBN/EAN: 9783337218232

Printed in Europe, USA, Canada, Australia, Japan

Cover: Foto ©ninafisch / pixelio.de

More available books at **www.hansebooks.com**

THE NOTE ON ROMANTICISM
THE BIOGRAPHIES and the DE-
SCRIPTIONS OF THE PICTURES
are by WILLIAM ERNEST HENLEY.

THE ETCHINGS AND SKETCHES
are by WILLIAM HOLE A.R.S.A.
and PHILIP ZILCKEN The HAGUE.

THE ETCHING No. 108 IS THE GIFT
of BERNARDUS JOH. BLOMMERS.

MEMORIAL CATALOGUE

OF THE

FRENCH AND DUTCH

LOAN COLLECTION

Edinburgh International Exhibition 1886

EDINBURGH

Printed at the University Press by T. & A. CONSTABLE

and Published by DAVID DOUGLAS

1888

The Edition consists of 520 copies, of which Nos. 1 to 100 are large paper with Etchings on Japanese.

No. 384

CONTENTS.

A NOTE ON ROMANTICISM BY W. E. HENLEY,   *page* ix

POSTSCRIPT BY ONE OF THE COMMITTEE,   xxxvii

FRENCH PICTURES.

	PAGE		PAGE
COROT (6 Sketches),	1	MANCINI (1 Sketch),	47
COURBET,	10	METTLING (1 Sketch),	50
DAUBIGNY (4 Sketches),	13	MILLET (6 Sketches),	52
DECAMPS,	19	MONTICELLI (3 Sketches),	60
DELACROIX (1 Sketch),	21	ROUSSEAU (2 Sketches),	66
DIAZ (2 Sketches),	27	ROYBET (1 Sketch),	74
DUPRÉ (1 Sketch),	33	SWAN (1 Sketch),	75
FANTIN-LATOUR (1 Sketch),	36	TROYON (3 Sketches),	77
FRÈRE,	39	VINCELET,	82
INGRES,	41	VOLLON,	83
JACQUE,	43	ZIEM,	86
LEGROS (1 Sketch),	45		

DUTCH PICTURES.

	PAGE		PAGE
ARTZ,	91	MARIS, J. (5 Sketches), .	108
BLOMMERS,	92	MARIS, M. (5 Sketches), .	116
BOSBOOM (2 Sketches), .	93	MARIS, W. (1 Sketch),	124
CLAYS,	98	MAUVE (2 Sketches),	126
ISRAELS (3 Sketches).	99	MESDAG (1 Sketch),	129
JONGKIND,	105	NEUHUYS (1 Sketch),	131
LEYS, .	106	TER MEULEN,	133

ETCHINGS.

COROT.
		PAGE
Landscape with Rocks,	Ph. Zilcken	5
An Evening in Normandy,	W. Hole,	8

DIAZ.
Sunset: Autumn,	W. Hole,	29

DUPRÉ.
Pointe des Dunes,	Ph. Zilcken,	34

JACQUE.
Le Retour du Troupeau,	W. Hole,	44

MONTICELLI.
The Ravine,	W. Hole,	63

ROUSSEAU.
The Hunt,	W. Hole,	72

BLOMMERS.
Girl and Child,	B. J. Blommers,	92

BOSBOOM.
Interior of Church,	W. Hole,	96

ISRAELS.
The Sleeping Child,	Ph. Zilcken,	101

JACOBUS MARIS.
Landscape: Moonlight,	W. Hole,	113
Souvenir de Dordrecht,	Ph. Zilcken,	114

MATTHŸS MARIS.
Le Ménage,	Ph. Zilcken,	120
'He is Coming!'	W. Hole,	123

MAUVE.
Girl leading Cow,	Ph. Zilcken,	128

A NOTE ON ROMANTICISM

THE masters represented in the Loan Collection of French and Dutch Pictures formed by One of the Committee for the first International Exhibition held at Edinburgh were one and all the outcome of the Romantic revival in France. With the literary results of that movement the world has long been familiar: the genius of Hugo, Balzac, Dumas, Musset, George Sand commanded recognition almost from the outset. Its effect, however, upon the arts of sculpture, music, and painting has been realised only of recent years; and it has therefore been considered not improper to preface this Catalogue with a brief account of Romanticism in general, and especially of the way in which it worked upon the art of painting. The question is one of no particular nationality. The interests of art are the reverse of local or peculiar; and the time (it is hoped) is not far distant when the names of Corot and Millet will sound no more foreign in English ears than those of Raphael and Velasquez.

I

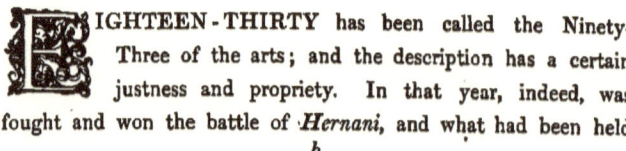EIGHTEEN - THIRTY has been called the Ninety-Three of the arts; and the description has a certain justness and propriety. In that year, indeed, was fought and won the battle of *Hernani*, and what had been held

a revolt was recognised and proclaimed a revolution. Too much has been made of the affair, no doubt: the interest was mainly one of style, the hero was a representative man of letters, the memory is one that literary men have united to exalt and cherish. The truth is, of course, that the work of reform was as good as done. Balzac had published *Les Chouans*, Dumas had created the type of the modern historical play in *Henri Trois et sa Cour*, Constable had appeared and conquered, Delacroix had exhibited the *Massacre de Scio* and the *Mort de Sardanapale*, Huet and Isabey had broken new ground in landscape, Rude and Barye were violating as they would the academical ideal of sculpture, Macready and Miss Smithson had been seen and heard in Shakespeare's own *Othello*, Frédérick was renowned both as the Macaire of *L'Auberge des Adrets* and the Georges de Germany of *Trente Ans*, the *Méditations* of Lamartine was almost an old book, Habeneck had founded the Conservatoire concerts, Berlioz was hard at work on the *Symphonie Fantastique*, Sainte-Beuve had produced the famous *Tableau Historique et Critique*, while Hugo himself had renewed and reinspired the lyric faculty of France; so that, it may fairly be argued, in the matter of essentials not much remained to accomplish or essay. But when all is said, the occasion was momentous enough. The poet's claim amounted to nothing less than the prescriptive right of every artist to be as lawless as Shakespeare; his opponents urged that there was no salvation outside Racine and Boileau; and for five-and-forty nights the question was debated before and by the audiences of the Théâtre-Français. The result was what we know. *Hernani* has been called "an undeveloped opera," and in sober truth is rather a five-act lyric than a drama. But it took its place beside *Le Cid*; and there was demonstrated with every circumstance of publicity —what is equally true of Sophocles and M. Zola, of the *Iliad* and the *Légende des Siècles*—that in the composition of a work of art the individual genius of the artist counts for at least as much as the principles on which he has wrought.

What, indeed, is called Romanticism—the change, that is to say, in the material, the treatment, and the technical methods and ideals of art which was operated in the France of Charles x. and Louis-Philippe—was the outcome of a generation rich in strenuous and potent individualities. The great emotions of the Republic and the Empire had induced such an efflorescence of temperament and genius as the world has not often seen. It were beside my purpose to speak of its impact upon war and politics and science; I have but to consider it in its relation to the arts. The fact is one that might easily be driven to death; but I may begin by noting, that the inspiration of the time was wholly Napoleon's, and that it might be argued with some show of reason, that Romanticism was as much a part of his legacy as the *Code* itself, or the memory of Austerlitz and Montmirail. It is at any rate certain that the period of his ascendancy was a time of intense and peculiar suffering, that it was also a time of enormous enterprise and achievement, and that it was under the pressure of these conditions that the men and women of the Romantic revival—"cette grande génération de Mille-Huit-Cent-Trente," says Gautier, with honourable pride, "qui marquera dans l'avenir, et dont on parlera comme d'une des époques climatériques de l'esprit humain"—were engendered and conceived. It is only the few who date from earlier days. Chateaubriand, "le Sachem du Romantisme en France," its archetype in insincerity of sentiment and splendour of style, was born in 1768, three years before Walter Scott; Béranger, Ingres, and Charles Nodier followed in 1780; Habeneck in 1781; Lamennais and Rude in 1782 and 1783; Mlle. Georges, the original Lucrèce Borgia and Marguerite de Bourgogne, in 1786;

David d'Angers in 1789—a year after Byron; Géricault, Scribe, and Lamartine—with Meyerbeer, whose share in Romanticism is large enough almost to make a Frenchman of him—in 1791; Charlet in 1792; and Lablache in 1793. All these, however, were the elders of the movement, the more active and characteristic forces of which began to be in one or other of the twenty years between the commencement of 1795—which saw the birth of the historian Thierry and the sculptor Barye—and the end of 1814—which gave Prince Bismarck to Germany, and to France the painter of the *Angélus* and the *Berger au Parc*. Corot came in 1796; Thiers and Pierre Leroux, in 1797; Michelet and Méry in 1798; Balzac, Halévy, Henri Monnier, Alfred de Vigny, and Eugène Delacroix in 1799. Frédérick Lemaître, the hero of half a hundred memorable dramas, was, like Heine, "one of the first men of the century"; his rival, Bocage, and his "female," Marie Dorval—the Dorval of *Antony, Chatterton, Angélo, Marion Delorme*—were, like *Atala*, the offspring of 1801, as were Ernest Littré, the satirist Gavarni, and the admirable comedian Lafont. Next year was the year of the *Génie du Christianisme*, and among its births were those of Victor Hugo, Lacordaire, Froment Meurice, Eugène Isabey, Camille Flers, and Alexandre Dumas; those of Berlioz, Mérimée, Quinet, Decamps, and Tony Johannot, were registered in 1803; those of Delphine Gay and Aurore Dudevant, of Nestor Roqueplan, Raffet, Paul Huet, Sainte-Beuve, the musician Hippolyte Monpou—and at Stockholm Marie Taglioni—are credited to 1804. In 1805, connate with our own Disraeli, a *romantique* of the first magnitude in his way and day, were the poets Auguste Barbier and Gérard de Nerval, the painter Eugène Devéria—for a year or two "le Véronèse de la France"—and the novelist Charles de Bernard. In 1806 were born the tenor Duprez and Louis Boulanger, artist in lithography of a once famous *Ronde du*

Sabbat, and in colour of a once famous *Mazeppa*; in 1808, Maria Malibran, the painter Diaz, and the actor-sculptor Mélingue, the original D'Artagnan, the original Chicot, the original Henri de Lagardère; in 1810, Hégésippe Moreau, Montalembert, Constant Troyon, Alfred de Musset, and the incomparable draughtsman and caricaturist Honoré Daumier; in 1811, the year of Thackeray and Liszt, Théophile Gautier and Jules Dupré; in 1812, Théodore Rousseau in Paris and Charles Dickens at Portsmouth; and in 1813, with Richard Wagner—in whose work the Romantic tendency assumed its most extravagant expression—at Leipzig, the dramatist Félicien Mallefille and Louis Veuillot, the polemist and journalist. The list, which might be made longer, is already long enough; but its variety is even more remarkable than its length. In the intellectual history of the world it would, I apprehend, be difficult, if not impossible, to name an epoch in which so many men attained to such eminence in so many of the arts at once. We think of the Age of Pericles as the age of sculpture, of the Age of Elizabeth as the age of the poetic drama. Romanticism is as it were a symphony for the full orchestra of the arts. Good work was done in poetry and drama, history and fiction, painting, sculpture, and journalism, singing and acting, symphony and opera and song; and though much of it has perished, a great deal has lived to be ranked with the best of its kind.

It is, perhaps, a paradox, that the great First Cause of Romanticism was Napoleon; it would probably be safer, as my friend Mr. Saintsbury has suggested, for "Napoleon" to read "the ferment of national spirit and the stimulus of national glory all through the revolutionary period." In any case, it is a truth that he was wholly unconscious of his work. Being an Italian, he was also in his way an artist. That he liked good acting, and was deeply interested in the theatre, is shown by his patronage of

Talma and Georges and Mars, and, above all, by the famous
"Décret de Moscou"; that he was capable of having an opinion of
his own in music, by his squabbles with Cherubini and his notice
of Spontini and Lesueur. He could give David a start in painting;
he may almost be said to have created Gros; while his first
proceeding after the conquest of Italy was to make a clean
sweep of all the pictures and statues in the peninsula that were
worth stealing. He had a vigorous literary instinct and an
admirable sense of style, or he could not have written the series
of bulletins and proclamations which Sainte-Beuve, if I remember
aright, regarded as in some sort the nearest approach to a great
national epic in the literature of France. But he was a
despot first and an artist afterwards; and as a despot he had
no love for new ideas and no tolerance for intellectual independence. He cared nothing for Chateaubriand, Benjamin
Constant he dismissed and disgraced, he exiled and suppressed
Mme. de Stael. That, as he boasted, he would have made
Corneille a senator is possible; that he would first of all have
muzzled him is absolutely certain. He could turn out generals
and administrators by the dozen; but it was a different matter
when he came to deal with art and artists. His reign was not
altogether barren of masterpieces, it is true: it was for him that
Gros had painted the series of heroic pictures which includes
the *Pestiférés de Jaffa*, the *Aboukir*, and the decorations in
the cupola of the Panthéon; it was under his auspices, and at
his Académie de Musique that Spontini produced the *Vestale*
and the *Fernand Cortez*, and Lesueur his *Bardes*; it was to a
public of his subjects that Chateaubriand addressed his *Atala*
and his *Génie du Christianisme*, and Mme. de Stael her *Corinne*
and her memorable *De l'Allemagne*. None of these things was
old-fashioned; on the contrary, their tendencies were boldly experimental, and they were fresh in sentiment and peculiar in

effect. But, for all that, as far as art is concerned, the France which was handed over to the Bourbons after Waterloo had the look of so much dead land. As exemplified in the practice of the great artists of the past—in the tragedies of Corneille and Racine, the comedies of Molière and Regnard, the prose of Sévigné and La Bruyère, the familiar verse of Voltaire and La Fontaine, the discourses of Bossuet and Fénelon, the novels of Lesage, the noble canvasses of Claude and the Poussins, the music of Gluck, the histrionics of Lecouvreur and Baron and Lekain—the classic convention is in the highest degree admirable. Plainly its qualities are dignity of style, lucidity in expression, reticence and elevation of sentiment; plainly it necessitates the cult of elegance of form and the attainment of a masterly sobriety of method; plainly it is incompatible with the mannerisms which are offensive because they are merely personal. The reverse of the medal is less pleasing in design. The classic convention, it is evident, is as easily abused as it is hard to handle with an approach to perfection. Selection, its distinguishing principle, can only be exercised with profit upon material at once abundant in quantity and of sterling excellence in kind. Given a man of genius who is also a great artist, and we get such results as *Cinna*, and *Armide*, and the *Arcadia*; given a man of talent who is also an accomplished craftsman, and we have to be content with the pictures of Girodet and the alexandrines of the Abbé Delille. During the early years of the Restoration Girodet was reckoned a master, while the memory of the Abbé Delille was cherished by all true children of the Muse. Classicism, in other words, lay on the arts like not a bloom, but a blight. It was the official faith. It was enthroned at the Académie, it governed the Théâtre-Français, it possessed the Salon, it inspired the press, and through the press it shaped the course of public opinion. There are hints of it in Hugo's earliest *Odes*, in Lamartine's *Méditations*, in Géricault's strange and daring masterpiece itself.

The reforming inspiration was not developed, but transmitted. The time had been when, as an integral part of French influence, the classic formula was paramount all over Europe. As we have seen, however, it was fallen into the last stage of senile decrepitude even in France, while in Germany and England it had been swept utterly away. The first to rise against it was Germany, where the modern tendency had achieved what is so far its loftiest and most heroic expression in the instrumental music of Beethoven, and where the study of other perfections than those recognised in Boileau and La Harpe had resulted in the hands of such men as Goethe and Schiller, Bürger and Lessing and Tieck, Uhland and the Schlegels, in the creation of a national literature. Its adoption in England, where the activity of Shakespeare and Milton had never been altogether suspended, was easy and swift. Goethe had owed his awakening to the authority of Shakespeare; and it was the first-fruits of this inspiration—the *Goetz von Berlichingen* of 1771-3—that, with Iffland's plays and the ballads of Bürger, determined the destiny of Walter Scott, and so called into action the fiery genius of Byron. With these two at work, the act of change was soon accomplished. Of course they did not stand alone. Beside them were Crabbe, Wordsworth, Keats, and Shelley in poetry: with Hazlitt and Lamb in criticism, Coleridge in criticism and poetry, Edmund Kean in histrionics, and Turner, Constable, and De Wint in painting. But I think it may fairly be said, that the master forces of the Romantic revival in England were Scott and Byron. They were the vulgarisers (as it were) of its most human and popular tendencies; and it is scarce possible to exaggerate the importance of the part they bore in its evolution. In their faults and in their virtues, each was representative of one or other of the two main tendencies of his time. With his passion for what is honourably immortal in the past, his immense and vivid instinct of the picturesque, his inexhaustible humanity, his magnificent moral health, his abounding and infallible sense of the eternal realities of life, Scott was an incarnation of chivalrous and manly duty; while Byron, with his swaggering cynicism, his passionate regard for passion, his abnormal capacity of defiance, and that overbearing and triumphant individuality which made him, as has been said, one of the greatest elemental forces ever felt in literature—Byron was the very genius of revolt. Each in his way became an European influence, and between them they made Romanticism in France. The men of 1830, it is true, were not altogether deaf to the voices, or blind to the examples, of certain among their own ancestors—Ronsard, for instance, and the poets of the Pleiad, Rousseau and Saint-Simon, André Chénier and Bernardin de Saint-Pierre, Villon and Montaigne and Rabelais. But it is a principal characteristic of them, that they were anxiously cosmopolitan. They quoted more languages than they knew. They were on intimate terms with all the names in the aesthetic history of the world. They boxed the compass for inspiration, and drank it in at every point upon the card :—from Goethe, Schiller, Hoffmann, Heine, Iffland, Beethoven, Weber in Germany; from Dante, Titian, Rossini, Piranesi, Gozzi, Benvenuto in Italy; from Constable, Turner, Maturin, Lawrence, Shakespeare, Thomas Moore in England; from Calderon, Goya, Cervantes, the poets of the *Romancero*, in Spain. But all these were later in time than Byron and Scott, or were found less potent and less moving when they came. Thus the *Faust* of Goethe was not translated until 1823; the *Eroica* of Beethoven, whose work was long pronounced incomprehensible and impossible of execution, was only heard in 1828, the real *Freischütz* some thirteen years after ; while

Macready's revelation of Shakespeare, till then not much except a monstrous and mysterious name, was contemporaneous with Habeneck's of Beethoven. Scott and Byron, on the other hand, had but to be known to be felt, and they were known almost at once. I have said, that the effect of Romanticism was a revolution in the technique, the material, and the treatment of the several arts. I do not think I affirm too much in adding, that but for Scott and Byron the revolution would have come later than it did, and would, as regards the last two, have taken a different course when it came.

As in England, the first in the field was Scott. When he attended the Congress of Paris in 1815 the fame of his verse had preceded him; his novels were freely imitated during the early Restoration; he was speedily accessible (1816-36) in translations—by Martin, Pichot, and Defauconpret—of which some fourteen hundred thousand volumes were sold in his lifetime alone. His generous and abounding influence was felt, indeed, with equal force by the average reader and the pensive poet. To say nothing of *Cromwell*, which may well be referable in some sort to *Les Puritains d'Écosse* (which is, being interpreted, *Old Mortality*), one of Hugo's first attempts in drama was an *Amy Robsart* written in collaboration with Paul Foucher; Op. 1. of Berlioz is a *Waverley* overture; subjects from *Ivanhoe* and *Quentin Durward* occur with delightful frequency in the catalogue of Delacroix; the origin of such notable departures in romantic prose as *Notre-Dame*, the *Chronique de Charles IX.*, and *Isabelle de Bavière*, and of such achievements in romantic verse as the *Pas d'Armes du Roi Jean*, is patent. Scott, indeed, was responsible for the historical element in Romanticism. He taught his pupils to be interested in the past, to admire and understand the picturesque in character and life, to look for romance in reality, and turn old facts to new and brilliant uses.

He was, no doubt, the author of "le jeune homme moyen-âge," and through him of a real phantasmagoria of castellans and high-born damozels, of rapiers and donjon keeps and long-toed shoes; but he has also to be credited with the inspiration of not a little of what is best and most enduring among the results of the revolution. It must not, however, be forgotten—it cannot be too constantly recalled—that Romanticism was above all an effect of youth. A characteristic of the movement—which has been called "an aesthetic barring-out"—was the extraordinary precocity of its heroes. The *Dante et Virgile* and the *Radeau de la Méduse*, the *Odes et Ballades* and *Hernani*, *Antony* and *Henri Trois et sa Cour*, *Rolla* and the *Nuits*, the *Symphonie Fantastique* and the *Comédie de la Mort*, are all masterpieces of their kind, and are all the work of men not thirty years old. Byron is pre-eminently a young men's poet; and upon the heroic boys of 1830—greedy of emotion, intolerant of restraint, contemptuous of reticence and sobriety, sick with hatred of the platitudes of the official convention, and prepared to welcome as a return to truth and nature inventions the most extravagant and imaginings the most fantastic and far-fetched—his effect was little short of maddening. He was fully translated as early as 1819-20; and the modern element in Romanticism—that absurd and curious combination of vulgarity and terror, cynicism and passion, truculence and indecency, extreme bad-heartedness and preposterous self-sacrifice—is mainly his work. You find him in Dumas's plays, in Musset's verse, in the music of Berlioz, the pictures of Delacroix, the novels of George Sand. He is the origin of *Antony* and *Rolla*, of *Indiana* and the *Massacre de Scio*, of Berlioz's *Lélio* and Frédérick's *Macaire*, as Scott is that of *Bragelonne*, and the *Croisés à Constantinople*, and Michelet's immortal history.

As regards these elements, then, Romanticism was largely an

importation. As regards technique—the element of accomplishment and style—it was not. Of this the inspiration was native, the revolution operated from within. The men of 1830 were craftsmen born: they had the genius of their material. The faculty of words, sounds, colours, situations was innate in them; their use of it is always original and sound, and is very often of exemplary excellence. It is hard to forgive—it is impossible to overlook—the vanity, the intemperance, the mixture of underbred effrontery and sentimental affectation, by which a great deal of their work is distinguished. Such qualities are "most incident" to youth, we know; and in a generation drunk with the divinity of Byron they were inevitable. Bad manners, however, are offensive at any age, and the convinced *romantique*, as he was all-too prone to make a virtue of loose morals, was all-too apt to make a serious merit of unmannerliness. But good breeding and moral perfectness are not what one expects of the convinced *romantique*: to do so were like looking to Mr. Meredith for plain English, or to Mr. Howells for the gallantry and the romance of *Bragelonne*. What we ask of him—what we get of him without asking—is craftsmanship, and craftsmanship of the true immortal type. Hugo may have written a whole library of nonsense; but in verse, at least, his technical imagination was Shakespearean. The moral tone of *Antony* is detestable; but it remains the most complete and masterly expression of some essentials of drama which the century has seen. The melodic inspiration of (say) *Harold en Italie* and the *Messe des Morts* may, or may not, be strained and thin; but if only his orchestration be considered, the boast of their author, "J'ai pris la musique instrumentale où Beethoven l'a laissée," is found to be neither impudent nor vain. In a sense, then, it is fitting enough that the year of *Hernani* should be accepted as a marking date in the story of the revival. If it have nothing else, assuredly

Hernani has style; and the "eternising influence" of style is such, that, if all save their technical achievement were forgotten, the masters of 1830 would still be remembered as great artists.

The revolution triumphed, and with reason; but its triumph was very far from being absolute. It proved the greater *romantiques* to be men of singular strength and genius; it cleared the air of a deadly mist of prejudice and affectation; on every hand it opened up new paths, and discovered new horizons; above all, it gave to art a world of novel and appropriate material. But it did not demonstrate the inherent and intrinsic superiority of the new convention to the old. On this point, indeed, the argument for Romanticism appears to me to have broken down. In 1831, for instance, the receipts of the Théâtre-Français ran down one night to something over seventy francs; in 1837, when Bocage and Frédérick were at the height of their fame, they ran up again to close on two hundred sterling a night; with Rachel on the stage the classic repertory—Corneille, Racine, even Voltaire—was found as great and moving as ever. This was in the hey-day of the movement, and I give the fact for what it is worth. It may be taken in conjunction with the view, that perhaps the most perfect of all the results of the revival is the art of Corot, in which the style is that of a pupil of Claude, while the matter is that of an inheritor of Constable. It remains to note—though this is rather interesting than important—that the Romanticism of 1830 was never an official success. The rancour and the obloquy with which its beginnings were received, are in strange contrast with the good temper and (on the whole) the fairness which marked the course of the anti-classical movement in England, where Byron was the spoiled child of Gifford, and there was none much readier than Hazlitt the arch-whig to do justice upon the arch-tory Scott. They may be said, I think, to have pursued it until the end. Dumas was never of the Académie, nor were Gautier and Balzac, while Barye had to wait for the distinction till he was close on seventy years old. Berlioz was rejected more than once, and so was Eugène Delacroix: only, it would seem, because they knew the weight and value of official recognition, did they stoop to have their way. Quite late in life the one was selling his pictures for a few pounds apiece, while the other, after a career of poverty and glory, was at last obliged to burke his ideas as they came, lest they should grow into symphonies which it would have made him bankrupt to produce. It seems fair to conclude, that, the development of some brilliant and profitable notorieties notwithstanding, Romanticism was no more a popular than an official success.

II

NOT many men have exercised so potent and enduring an influence in art as Louis David. His effect upon the painter of the *Pestiférés de Jaffa* is typical of his authority in life. In 1823, David being then in exile at Brussels, Gros was at the very top of his fame. He was a Baron, a Knight of the Order of Saint Michael, and a member of the Institute; he was high in favour with the King, as he had been with the Emperor; he was Professor of Painting at the École des Beaux-Arts; he had taken over David's School, and was known for the kindest and most competent of teachers. Yet it is told of him, that when he conveyed to David the gold medal struck in honour of the master by his former pupils, he no sooner caught sight of the house in which the old despot had taken up his quarters, than he was seized with a passion of terror and respect, and had to sit down in the street, and collect his spirits, ere he could bring himself to knock at the door. Nor was this the worst.

He was the earliest of the *romantiques*; he had formulated a convention, evolved a style, demonstrated the possibilities of a vast amount of new material, and shown the way to regions unknown or inaccessible before; his greater works had already taken rank with the masterpieces of the French school; yet when David wrote to him, that he was to give over the painting of buttons and cocked hats, look up his Plutarch, and enrich the world with a real historical picture, he obeyed his instructions to the letter, and returned in all simplicity and good faith to the practice of the heroic nude. He was reviled as a renegade and denounced as a reactionary; the revolution he had initiated was triumphing all along the line; he ceased to be able to sell his pictures. But, though David was dead, he went on conning his Plutarch, and painting exactly as he would have done had David been alive and at his elbow. In the June of 1835, after a last colossal failure at the Salon, he drowned himself in the Seine. That, however, was only the end of the man. The artist had committed suicide some fourteen years before, and had done it by David's orders.

With classicism as the official cult, and a disciplinarian of the stamp of David in authority, the chance of heresy, it might be thought, was insignificant enough. But in truth the beginnings of Romanticism were easy. In all the arts the expression of heterodox views appears, at the inception of the movement, to have been the reverse of unwelcome. In literature the success of *Atala* was instant and complete; in music the experiments of Spontini and Lesueur were considered with enthusiasm. It was not otherwise in painting, though here the iron will of David, his intense and rigid personality, his admirable accomplishment, and his immense authority, were felt as direct and immediate influences. He had started as an imitator of Boucher; had studied the antique in Rome (1775-80) under Vien; had returned to Paris an incarnation of that interest in the work of the Greeks and Romans among whose first fruits is the *Laocoon* of Lessing; had painted the *Bélisaire*, the *Serment des Horaces*, the *Mort de Socrate*; and had so completely changed the fashion of French art that his pupils (it is said) made studies on the backs of stray canvasses and drawings signed by Antoine Watteau. That solemn mockery of things Roman, which was a characteristic of the Revolution, appeared to him in the light of a great and noble reality. He carried it from painting into politics, and back again from politics into painting; he believed in it as the outward and visible sign of civic and artistic virtue; much of its vogue with the general may be attributed to his personal influence and example. The suppression of the Académie de Peinture was largely his work, as were a number of changes and reforms besides; he began, but never finished, an enormous picture of the Session of the Tennis Court,—"famed *Séance du Jeu de Paume*," as Carlyle calls it; he was responsible, among other abominations in pasteboard or in plaster, for the hideous and colossal allegory which— "imposante par son caractère de force et de simplicité"—should represent, to the admiration of all good patriots, "l'image du peuple Français" defying the world from a pedestal composed of "les effigies des rois et les débris de leurs vils attributs"; he was master of the revels to the Republic and gentleman-usher to the newly invented Supreme Being; in a style and temper which may be said to have made him a *romantique* before the fact, he painted the posthumous portraits of Lepelletier Saint-Fargeau and Marat; he idolised Robespierre, with whom he offered (publicly) to share the Socratic hemlock. After the 9th Thermidor he was violently denounced in the Convention; stigmatized as a "vile usurper" and a "despot of the arts"; suspended from his service on the committees; arrested more than once, and kept in durance for months at a time; and saw his *Marat Expirant* and his *Lepelletier* removed in infamy from their place in the Panthéon. But at last he regained his liberty, and in no great while he had regained his credit also. He painted his *Enlèvement des Sabines*; he was made a member of the Institute; his studio —from which, at one time or another, he sent out such disciples as Gros, Ingres, Drouais, Gérard, the elder Isabey, Schnetz, Granet, Girodet, Rude, Gudin, David d'Angers, and Léopold Robert—was thronged with pupils. His rivals were also his imitators; his ascendancy was so real, and his dictatorship so absolute that Prudhon, as late as 1810, was obliged to change his style, and paint an heroic allegory for the Salon, "pour obtenir," says Delécluze, "la faveur d'être placé au nombre de ce qu'on appelle les peintres d'histoire." But if David was strong, Napoleon was stronger still. It was a feature of his campaign against the future, that his work should receive an adequate pictorial expression; and David, whom he met and subjugated at the outset of his career, was among the means he used to his end. He began by sitting to the painter for two portraits: one the magnificent sketch (unfinished) of the General of the Army of Italy; the other that one of the First Consul on horseback which is known as *Napoleon Crossing the Alps*. Afterwards he appointed David his painter in ordinary; obliged him to remember that he was the artist of the *Marat Expirant* and the *Serment du Jeu de Paume* as well as of the *Sabines* and the *Bélisaire*; ordered him out of the world of sculpture-in-paint he lived to represent; and made him put aside his *Leonidas*, and set to work on the *Couronnement de Napoléon* and the *Distribution des Aigles*. David was a born tyrant, but hero-worship was a necessity of life with him. He adored Napoleon, as he had adored Marat and Robespierre. He could refuse his idol nothing. He appears to have uttered not so much as a murmur against the popularity of those pictures of buttons and cocked hats with which, during year after year of the Empire, the Salon was crowded. It was not until his master and himself were banished men, and the splendid pageant of Napoleonism had vanished like a dream, that he took up his testimony against them, and reminded his old pupil that the way of salvation lay through Plutarch's *Lives*.

David's concessions were, however, as those of one royalty to another and greater. It was far otherwise with Gros. Without the Napoleonic inspiration he might never have deviated into originality at all. A favourite with his master and with Mme. Vigée-Lebrun, he had escaped, with David's help, from the Paris of the Terror, and betaken himself to the Italy of the First Campaign; and at Milan he had fallen in with Josephine. It was the beginning of fame and fortune. Josephine was too generous and impulsive to do good by halves. She took up the young painter with enthusiasm; introduced him to her husband; got him commissions — the *Bonaparte à la Bataille d'Arcole* among them; and ended by making him one of the Committee of Selection appointed to furnish Paris with the treasures of Florence and Rome. One consequence of this function was that Gros became a worshipper of Michelangelo; another, that he served under Massena in the Defence of Genoa, and saw war face to face. Returning to Paris (1801), he was chosen to paint for the State a picture of the Battle of Nazareth. The work was begun, but never finished. It would necessarily have been an apotheosis of Junot, and the First Consul, who had his own opinion as to the unique and proper subject for such distinctions, was not slow to cancel the commission. He replaced it by another, with a theme in which he took an interest of a different kind; and in 1804 Gros exhibited the renowned *Pestiférés de Jaffa*. Its effect was triumphant: it was hung round with laurel and palm; it was purchased for the

State for as much as 16,000 francs—in those days a magnificent honorarium; the painters, Vien and David at their head, gave a banquet in its honour. Its success was fully deserved: it invested an actuality with the dignity of heroic art, and it did this by means of a presentment of the truth, imaginative indeed, but literal and direct enough to convey an intense suggestion of reality; it was eminently personal in subject, treatment, and style, and it was also a revelation of material. Its tendencies were accentuated, and its conclusions were stated more resolutely, and in some sort more brilliantly, in the *Aboukir* of 1806 and in the *Eylau* of 1809, the one a picture of war in the very act, the other of war as it looks next day. It was impossible that from such work there should not ensue a vast amount of experiment and change: the sentiment was too novel and affecting, the material too rich, the effect too striking and complete. In the *Pestiférés*—the *Atala* of painting—Romanticism was formulated and suggested; with the *Aboukir* and the *Eylau* it became inevitable. Gros, as we have seen, was presently to deny his work, and go over to the enemy; he was weak of will and deficient in self-confidence, and it is doubtful if he realised the value, or perceived the possibilities, of his discovery. But the inspiration of which, whether consciously or unconsciously, he had been the vehicle, had long since passed into the common stock, and become public property. Ten years after the *Eylau* Géricault, who had forced his way to the front as early as 1812, exhibited the *Radeau de la Méduse*. Like his friend and fellow-worker, Delacroix, whose *Dante et Virgile* was itself but four years off, Géricault was a pupil of Guérin, but a follower of Gros. Plainly, therefore, his was a fertilising as well as a creative influence. The inception of the movement was his; and it was also his to determine the direction of the most active and potent agencies of its second phase.

Géricault had lived and worked in England (it is told of him, that he was profoundly impressed by the great romantic landscape of Turner); he was splendidly gifted and admirably trained; he was full of daring, energy, ambition, a born leader of men. But he died at thirty-three, his work—though he had done enough for fame—no more than begun, and his measure not stated, but barely indicated; and the conduct of the movement, which had by this time become militant and progressive, devolved upon his friend and disciple Eugène Delacroix. In line with him were artists of the stamp of Bonington (another Gros man) and Decamps, Scheffer and Delaroche, Boulanger and Devéria, and in another branch of art Isabey, Huet, Troyon, and Camille Flers. They were good men in their way, and they did good work, each after his kind. But the strongest and the most representative of all was Delacroix; and by virtue no less of his qualities than his aims he was soon the chief of the advance. But while he was the hero of the rebel camp, he was the horror of the other. His first picture had the honour to be described as the work of a drunken broom; his second was denounced as a deliberate attempt to establish the divinity of the Ugly; he got a commission from the Chief of the State, and he was requested to make the work as unlike a Delacroix as possible; his famous "Voilà trente ans que je suis livré aux bêtes" is but a plain account of his career. The reason is not far to seek. For one thing his message was original and disturbing, and for another his manner of utterance was singularly individual and new. The natural bias of the romantic artist is towards exaggeration and irrelevance. He must suggest too much, or he cannot believe that he has said enough; he bewilders by sheer excess of expressiveness. With Delacroix the aim and end of painting was the representation of, not beauty but, emotion. Like most of the men of his generation, he held, at least in the beginning, that passion must be not measureable, careful of form, attentive to deportment, eternally conscious of the rules of good breeding, but simply passionate—passionate above all, passionate at any cost—and that nature is natural in proportion as it is violent. His sincerity was unimpeachable, and he worked out his conviction as only a man of genius can. But to see that his art was great was given only to a few, while it was obvious to the many that the immediate effect of his visions of battle and murder and despair was the reverse of anodyne. Moreover, his style was one that lent itself to caricature. His qualities remained inimitable, but to practise his defects was easy; and it came to pass that loose drawing was quoted as a characteristic of style, and false colour as a sign of genius, while a horrible subject was a proof of poetry. "Le romantisme mal entendu," Heine wrote in 1831, "a infecté les ateliers de France; en conséquence du principe fondamental de cette doctrine *chacun s'efforce de peindre autrement que les autres, ou, pour parler le langage à la mode, de faire sortir son individualité.*" Five years after came the famous Salon of 1836. The Classics awoke to a sense of the position, and realised, confusedly but with a certain vividness, that Romanticism—like Impressionism to-day—was often another name for ignorance and a standing apology for ineptitude. They were in office, of course; and confounding good with bad, the reality and the sham, they resolved to strike *pro aris et focis*—for careful drawing and decorous colour. They shut and barred their doors upon Rousseau; they rejected work by Delacroix, Huet, Marilhat, the sculptor of the *Lion écrasant un Boa*. It must be owned that their exasperation, however crudely and intemperately expressed, was not ill-founded.

The chosen field of Romanticism in this stage of its development was drama. A return to nature in general, it was a return to human nature in particular. Géricault, Delacroix, Horace Vernet, Ary Scheffer, Charlet, Decamps, Boulanger, Gigoux, the Johannots and Devérias, Raffet and Daumier and Gavarni, were all artists in the figure; and it was in figure painting that the first great victories were gained. In the department of landscape, where the noblest work of the revival was presently to be done, there was not at first much fighting. The art was not yet popular; the sentiment had still to become a part of the general consciousness. The style in vogue was that of Valenciennes, who was born two years after David, and who operated in landscape a parallel reform to that effected by Vien and his illustrious pupil in the pictorial treatment of the figure. He classicised the art, that is to say: obliterating the traces alike of Watteau and of Joseph Vernet, he laid out the world in backgrounds for a populace of heroes and heroines improved from those of Plutarch by a long course of second-rate French tragedy. The result was learned and pompous; it had the true geometrical feeling, and was rich in the emphasis of archaeology and the eloquence of perspective; but it was also jejune, insignificant, and profoundly dull. At the worst of times the effect of such work as (say) the Valenciennes in the Louvre—*Cicéron, étant questeur en Sicile, découvre le tombeau d'Archimède, que les Syracusains assuraient ne pas posséder sur leur territoire* is its highly respectable name—could hardly have been exciting. Valenciennes and his followers, indeed, were only the small change of Claude and the Poussins; and the public was so far indifferent to their results that it was not at once seduced into knowing or caring anything about the proceedings of their assailants. Landscape is not a natural intoxicant. That experiments in the use of such material as the facts of massacre and shipwreck were passionately admired and as passionately resented, is not surprising: they belong to experience, they are a part of the fabric of life, their interest is dreadfully representative. To do as much with effects of light, and studies of cloud, and reminiscences of Asnières or Montmartre, was manifestly impossible. The material was uninteresting, being unfamiliar; the humanity was too purely subjective to be immediately apparent. Accordingly the beginnings of Romanticism in landscape were quiet and prosperous enough. Isabey exhibited at twenty, and gained a First Class medal with his first picture; Huet was medalled at twenty-nine, Troyon at twenty-five, Camille Roqueplan at twenty, Jules Dupré at twenty-two; Corot broke ground at the Salon of 1827, and never missed an exhibition till his death.

The intention of French landscape had all along been mainly decorative. The formula was found almost at starting, and in the hands of Nicolas Poussin (1594-1665), Claude Gellée (1600-1682), and Gaspar Dughet (1613-1675), a culmination was attained which is comparable in its way with Raphael's design and the painting of Velasquez. It may be described as a presentment, essentially imaginative and heroic, of certain of the greater aspects and the broader truths of nature. It is an art of luminous dawns and solemn dusks; its aërial architecture is vast in design and largely accurate in fact; its essentials are majesty of line, harmony of parts, dignity of conception, and a grandiose simplicity of sentiment and effect. It gave an ideal to art, and the strength of its example is not yet departed. But it had little to do with the common, work-a-day world whose pictorial quality, as perceived and developed by Rubens (1577-1640), is the whole material of modern landscape; and in France, where the realistic theory was not permitted to take root, and where in times comparatively recent the simple and passionate experiments of Georges Michel (1763-1842) were entirely ignored, its effect upon the art was the reverse of fortunate. In the work of Watteau (1684-1721), the landscape element, for all its suggestiveness, its mystery and charm, is an accessory; in that of Boucher (1704-1770) and his following, its function is unchanged, if its magic has departed; with Joseph Vernet (1714-1789), a pupil of the Italian pupils of Claude and Dughet, it began to be once more painted for itself, and to be touched with a serious spirit of observation and inquiry; with Valenciennes (1750-1819), and his tribe—Bidault, Michallon, Bertin, Aligny, and the rest—and the development of the *paysage historique*, it lost, as I have said, all touch with life, and fell, as it seemed, into a state of hopeless dotage. At this time, indeed, the art was at its lowest almost everywhere. The Italian school was dead of emphasis and affectation; in Flanders the seed of Rubens and the posterity of Brueghel (1568-1625) had both passed utterly away; in Holland, where the naturalistic principle had passed from culmination to culmination in the work of Van Goyen (1596-1666), Cuyp (1605-1691), Rembrandt (1607-1669), Ruysdael (1625-1682), Hobbema (1638-1709), there was now the silence of the void. Only in England was there anything of the ardour and the stress of life. There the two great influences had developed, one the tranquil and lovely art of Wilson (1714-1782), after the original the most complete and graceful expression of the Claude convention in existence, the other the brilliant and suggestive art of Gainsborough (1727-1788). Both were far in the past; but during the first quarter of the present century the men who had arisen in their room were doing even greater work than theirs. Crome (1769-1821) was following with singular strength, intelligence, and originality the lead of Meindert Hobbema, and in founding the Norwich school — Cotman, Vincent, John Crome, Stark, and the others—had established a new centre of activity; Girtin (1775-1802) and Cozens (1752-1799) had given a fresh start to water-colours; the astonishing and eccentric genius of Turner (1775-1851) was in mid-career; Constable (1776-1835) had found a new departure and developed a peculiar inspiration; Thomson of

Duddingston (1778-1840) was renewing and reinspiring the heroic convention of the Poussins by bringing it into nearer touch with nature, and informing it with his own sincere and ardent individuality; it was the epoch of De Wint (1784-1849), David Cox (1785-1859), Copley Fielding (1787-1855), Collins (1780-1847), Harding (1798-1863), to name but these. England had been the last to catch the spark. It was reserved for her to do with French landscape as with French literature, and count for not a little in the royalty of some of the kings of the art. And the chief agent in the work was Constable.

The thing, no doubt, was in the air. Romanticism was a return to more than human nature, after all. The tradition of J.-J. Rousseau and Bernardin de Saint-Pierre and the practice of Scott and Byron and Chateaubriand were making the landscape element an essential part of literature; and in painting the example of Rubens and the greater Dutchmen was found in intimate alliance with the authority of the Englishman Bonington and the initiative of Géricault. When in 1822 Paul Huet entered the *atelier* of Baron Gros, he had already painted for at least two years in the open air, and knew the Île Séguin as it were by heart. Huet was only one of many; so that when sowing-time came, and the sower came with it, the ground was well and widely prepared. How widely and how well was shown by the famous Salon of 1824. Among the exhibitors were Bonington, Lawrence, Thales and Copley Fielding, Harding, Wild, and Constable. Lawrence received the red ribbon; and gold medals were awarded to Bonington and Copley Fielding, who were represented, the one by five pictures and drawings, the other by no less than nine. The success of the year, however, was the Constables. They were three in number, the chief of them being the *Hay Wain* (originally purchased with two others for £250), which was presented not long since to the National Gallery by Mr. Henry Vaughan; and the

fury of discussion with which they were received was such as to
reach the ears and flatter the idiosyncrasy of the painter himself,
though (as one who gloried in the name of Briton) he regarded
the excitement of his hosts with a feeling of fine, solid, good-
humoured contempt. He received a gold medal; his pictures,
which at starting appear to have been badly hung, were removed to "prime places in the principal room"; their effect—
with that of the *White Horse*, exhibited next year at Lille and
elsewhere—was equally vivid and profound. In England a respectable failure then and for many years to come, Constable, at this
time a man of eight-and-forty, was in the plenitude of his genius
and accomplishment: his theory was not less individual and sound
than his practice, notwithstanding a certain lack of feeling for
elegance in the use of paint, was masterly. His merit was
twofold. He had looked long at truth with no man's eyes but
his own; and having caught her in the act, he had recorded his
experience in terms so personal in their masculine directness and
sincerity as to make his innovations irresistible. Never, save
by him, had so much pure nature been set forth in art.
He showed, that the sun shines, that the wind blows, that
water wets, that clouds are living, moving citizens of space,
that grass is not brown mud, that air and light are everywhere, that the trunks of trees are not disembodied appearances, but objects with solidity and surface. He proved
beyond dispute, that the tonality of a landscape is none the worse
for corresponding with something actually felt as existing in the
subject, and that the colours of things are not less representative
than their textures and their forms. He demonstrated, once
for all, the eternal principles of generalisation, and that a picture
lacking in the sense of weather and the feeling for mass, and in
which the small truths of a scene are preferred to its larger
and more characteristic elements, is so little in sympathy with

any romantic or poetic view of nature as to have no existence save as a more or less pleasing pattern. In other words, he was found to have carried the realistic ideal to a point so far ahead of the furthest reached by any of his predecessors, that the results he obtained, and the convention through which he obtained them, were practically new. What was more, they were new in the right way and to the right purpose. They tended to the cult of sincerity in observation and expression; they showed the use of a complete equipment; they foreshadowed a world of possibilities, the right of way through which was only to be won by close and patient intercourse with nature. They suggested the basis of an art which should deal broadly with man's impressions of the natural appearances of weather, atmosphere, and distance, and their correspondence with his moods. In fact, they were the beginnings of what has been called Romanticism in landscape. They did for it what Scott's novels and Byron's verse had done, or were doing, for fiction and poetry and the drama. They were the inspiration of what is fast coming to be recognised as the loftiest expression of modern painting; for not far behind them was the art of Rousseau, Daubigny, Dupré, Courbet, Diaz, and, above all, Millet and Corot—that art, in fact, which was the staple of the Loan Collection catalogued in this book.

III

MOST of the masters who are responsible for the revival of art in Holland—MM. Jongkind, Artz, Jacobus Maris, Mauve, Clays, and Josef Israels—are Paris-trained. This is, perhaps, another way of saying, that, like ourselves of late, though for very different reasons—chief among them, perhaps, the want of an Oxford Graduate in Dutch literature, and the absence

of a Turner in Dutch painting—they have read their Constable in
a French translation. Of course this must not be taken literally.
It will be fairer to say, that the inspiration of the modern Dutchmen is derived in part from the later and greater Romanticists, and
in part from their own renowned ancestors. They have been wise
enough to borrow; but they have been strong enough to turn
their acquisition to uses at once individual and national. It is
difficult, for instance, to believe of Josef Israels, that in the absence of J.-F. Millet he would be the painter-poet of poverty that
he is; that in Johannes Bosboom and Matthÿs Maris, though their
work is poles apart, there is not a certain touch of Corot; that
Jacobus Maris would have looked at nature with the same eyes,
or recorded his impressions with the same vigorous felicity, had
he lacked the example of the whole great school. But, this to
the contrary, the art of all these men is largely and sincerely
national. It is not an exotic, but a plant home-sown and
home-grown and racy of the soil. The *Dordrecht* and the
Landscape : Moonlight of the present Catalogue are Dutch in cast
and sentiment as Hobbema's *Avenue*; with the strain of Corot
that is felt in the strange and peculiar fantasies of Matthÿs
Maris there is combined a certain admixture of the mystery, the
romance, the feeling for realities not of this world, which are
characteristics of the mighty genius of Rembrandt; Bosboom's
interiors are pure Holland; the sea- and river-scapes of Clays
and Jongkind and Mesdag are the direct descent of Van der
Neer and Van de Velde, as the cattle-pieces of Mauve and Willem
Maris are that of Berchem and Paul Potter. The work conceived
and done by One of the Committee was, no doubt, imperfect.
But, for all its lapses, it was fairly representative of the greatest
and soundest development of modern painting; and this, I take
it, is exactly what it could not have been if it had failed to
include the present with the past. Both schools are native to the

A NOTE ON ROMANTICISM

core; but the one has followed and adapted where the other invented and explored. The foundation of both is the exact and faithful study of nature with a view to the passionate and romantic expression of experience; and in this way it comes to pass, that, as was shown, designedly or not, by One of the Committee, the true heirs and successors of the great Frenchmen of yesterday are the Dutchmen of to-day.

W. E. H.

POSTSCRIPT BY ONE OF THE COMMITTEE.

I wish to take advantage of this opportunity to acknowledge the kindness of the lenders of pictures, to whose generosity this Collection owed its existence. I think it unnecessary to repeat each name separately, and to make a selection might seem invidious where all were so free with their assistance. One exception however I feel bound to make in the case of Mr. Mesdag, who, though a stranger to me personally, came forward and gave his help.

I would also acknowledge my obligation to Mr. W. E. Lockhart, whose steady support enabled me to carry out my original plan.

That the Collection had many weak points I am painfully aware; but added to the mistakes from ignorance and want of experience on my part there were many difficulties arising from pressure and want of time. I cannot enter on the reasons I had for forming this Collection, as this would open up the entire field of art-criticism, a subject quite beyond my powers of expression. I may however state that it was a protest against much of the art-teaching of the present day, and an attempt to show that painting is an art which is not dependent on subject, but is complete in itself.

That this Collection was to a large extent confined to the French and Dutch painters was more an accident than the result of any preference on my part for these schools, as I believe that art is the gift of the individual, and not confined to any nation or locality.

NOTE

The Catalogue has been arranged alphabetically and re-numbered. The numbers in the original Catalogue are indicated by smaller figures, marked by a bracket, at the end of the description of each picture.

In the following pages the name JAMES STAAT-FORBES should have been printed JAMES STAATS FORBES.

FRENCH PICTURES

JEAN-BAPTISTE-CAMILLE COROT

1796—1875

BORN in Paris and educated at Rouen, Corot's first condition was that of a mercer's shopman; and he was six-and-twenty ere he could abandon it for Art. For five years in succession he took advantage of the festival of his father's birthday to plead for leave to follow his true vocation; and at last he won his cause, and was told to go and enjoy himself. His masters were Michallon (1796-1822) and Victor Bertin (1775-1822), both exponents of a convention in landscape analogous to, and proceeding from, the reform effected in historical and figure painting by Louis David (1748-1825). But from the first he painted steadily in the open air, in Italy—whither he went in 1826, and where he worked much with Aligny (1798-1871), "l'Ingres des arbres"—and elsewhere; and it is obvious that the example of Bonington and Paul Huet was no more without its effect upon him than the innovations announced in *The Hay Wain* and *The Lock on the Stour*. His first Salon was that of 1827; his last—he had died some two or three months before—that of 1875. Between the two are eight-and-forty years of incessant achievement, beginning with a period of failure (for Corot was a man of forty when he sold his first picture) and ending in a period of exceptional authority and fame. His official successes were few: like Balzac and Rousseau and Dumas he was excluded from the Institute; and he was twice refused the Medal of Honour, once in 1865, when it was carried away by Cabanel, and again in 1874, when it was awarded to Gérôme. But his popularity was immense. He was recognised for the rarest of artists, the most generous of men; and his last defeat was converted into a triumph by the presentation from his fellow-craftsmen of a subscription medallion in gold.

It amused him to paint, as it amused Dumas to write. The mere amount of his work is therefore considerable; and as he early attained to mastery, much of it is of singular merit. The *Danse de Nymphes*, the *Macbeth*, the *Homère et les Bergers*, the *Dante et Virgile*, the *Orphée*, the *Souvenir de Mortefontaine*, the *Matin à Ville d'Avray*, the *Saint Sebastien*, the *Joueur de Flûte*—to speak of these and fifty others of their kindred is to speak of work already classic: as *Las Lanzas* is classic, or Rembrandt's *Syndics*, or the *Arcadia* of Nicolas Poussin.

For Corot is a culmination. On his own ground he may challenge comparison with the greatest. He entered upon his career at a juncture when the classic convention, as developed by the descendants of the Poussins, was mined with decay and tottering to its fall, and as yet the forerunners of Romanticism were but groping their way towards new truths and new ideals; and it was his to unite in his art the best tendencies of both. It is to be supposed, as I have said, that his interest in pure nature and his perception of her inexhaustible suggestiveness were stimulated and determined by the revelations of certain artists who were at once his ancestors and his contemporaries; it is at any rate certain that he was himself as ardent and curious a student of facts as has ever painted, and that the basis of his art is a knowledge of reality as deep and sound as it is rich and novel. On the other hand, the essentials of classicism—composition, selection, treatment, the master quality of style—were his by genius and inheritance alike. In the artistic completeness of his formula he stands with Claude; in the freshness and novelty of his material with Constable and the moderns.

In him, however, there is much that is not Claude, and much more that is not Constable. There is Corot himself: a personality as rare, exquisite, and charming as has ever found expression in the plastic arts. He had that enjoyment of his medium for its own sake, denied—they tell us—even to Raphael; his sense of colour was infallibly distinguished and refined; his treatment of the best type. Given such means, and no more, and it is possible, as Courbet has shown, to do great things. To Corot, who painted as Jules Dupré declared, "pour ainsi dire, avec des ailes dans le dos," much more was possible. In his most careless work there is always art and there is always quality—a strain of elegance, a thrill of style, a hint of the unseen; while at his best he is not only the consummate artist, he is also the most charming of poets. If I remember aright, it is Cherbuliez who says of Mozart that he was "the only Athenian who ever wrote music." The phrase is a good one, it suggests so happily an ideal marriage of sentiment with style. With the substitution of landscape for music, it applies as happily to Corot. Corot is the Mozart of landscape.

1. **Storm on Sandhills.**

> A stretch of sand and grey-green herbage. On a hillock in the centre a leafless tree, storm-beaten and twisted. Beyond, a wild sky filled with grey wrack, but with glimpses of blue. In the foreground a woman, in whose cap is the one touch of red in all the picture. 32¾ by 44 inches. 83 centimètres by 1 mètre 12 centimètres. [1085.
>
> Lent by CONSTANTINE A. IONIDES, Esq., London.

2. Evening.

A grassy knoll with high trees against a quiet sky. In the distance a prospect of lake and hill. In the foreground a goat-herd piping to his flock. 36 by 28 inches. 91·50 by 71 centimètres. [1075.

Lent by D. MACDONALD, Esq., Strome.

3. Sunset.

A group of massive and sombre trees, relieved against water and a grey-blue sky with flecks of pearly cloud. 13 by 21½ inches. 33 by 54·50 centimètres. [1079.

Lent by JAMES DONALD, Esq., Glasgow.

4. Landscape: Early Morning.

On the left a lake, with cattle and figures and a group of trees. On the right the shore sweeps round a bay, with a white and red house on the far side. A harmony of quiet greens and blues. 12½ by 15½ inches. 32 by 39·50 centimètres. [1105.

Lent by ONE OF THE COMMITTEE.

5. **Landscape with Rocks.**

A road through a rocky country. On the right an overhanging tree. In the foreground a man. A delicate grey-blue sky, with level lines of cloud, lit by the rising sun. An effect in blue and grey. 15 by 24½ *inches.* 38 by 62 *centimètres.* [1083.

ETCHING. *Lent by* ARTHUR SANDERSON, Esq., Edinburgh.

6. **The Lake of Garda.**

A composition academical in treatment and elegant in effect. The scene is the banks of a lake. In the foreground, on the right, a great willow leaning leftwards, and in the middle distance a wooded promontory, with classic architecture, sloping down to the water. On the left, two slim trees, with a boatman drawing his bark ashore. The colour scheme, albeit a little cold, is one of extreme refinement. 22½ by 31¾ *inches.* 57 by 80·33 *centimètres.* [1154.

Lent by JAMES STAAT-FORBES, Esq., London.

7. **Lake and Landscape.**

A man boating on what is rather a mill-pond than a lake, with an environment of trees. On the far side a mill, reflected in the water. 14½ by 18 *inches.* 37 by 46 *centimètres.* [1108.

Lent by JAMES STAAT-FORBES, Esq., London.

8. Landscape.

A group of grey trees. On the left a sandy road, with a woman and two cows. In the distance a lake, with an effect of sunlight on the shore. 12¼ by 15¾ inches. 31 by 40 centimètres. [1090.

Lent by THE HON. MR. JUSTICE DAY, London.

9. The Lake.

In the foreground a meadow, with a woman herding cattle, and to the left a clump of trees on the water's edge. From the left middle distance a wooded hill, sloping down to the lake, with a line of white and red cottages. A delicate scheme of blue, grey, and pea-green. 12½ by 21½ inches. 31·75 by 54·50 centimètres. [1091.

Lent by DAVID ANDERSON, Esq., Glasgow.

10. An Old Castle.

A road with trees and a streamlet. On the right, in the middle distance, more trees with a ruined castle. In the foreground, on the left, a single figure. A scheme of cool, fresh, silvery greys and greens. 15¾ by 20¼ inches. 39 by 52 centimètres. [1087.

Lent by ONE OF THE COMMITTEE.

11. **In Arcadia.**

> A classic landscape, with a group of dancing nymphs. 16¼ by 29 inches. 41 by 73·50 centimètres. [1093.
>
> *Lent by* JAMES STAAT-FORBES, Esq., London.

12. **The Gloaming.**

> On the left a group of massive trees, with rocks. On the right a line of trees. 14½ by 18 inches. 37 by 46 centimètres. [1109.
>
> *Lent by* ONE OF THE COMMITTEE.

13. **The Woodcutters.**

> Early morning. A lake, seen from the shore. To the left and left centre, two trees, with yellow rocks sloping down to the water's edge. To the right a pile of buildings, crowning the slope of the bank. A scheme of cool greens and blues and pearly grey. 19¼ by 25 inches. 49 by 63·50 centimètres. [1137.
>
> *Lent by* JAMES DONALD, Esq.; Glasgow.

14. Moonlight.

A woodland river, with a group of bathing nymphs. 10½ by 14 *inches.* 26·50 by 35·50 *centimètres.* [1114.

Lent by H. W. MESDAG, Esq., The Hague.

15. By the Sea.

A sandy road across the dunes, leading down from a cottage in the background. On the left a hollow, with trees; on the right a patch of brambles. A scheme of delicate browns and silvery greys. 29 by 50 *inches.* 73·50 *centimètres by* 1 *mètre* 27·50 *centimètres.* [1132.

Lent by DANIEL COTTIER, Esq., London.

16. Landscape with Cows.

A stream, with cattle wading. On the right, on a rising ground, and relieved against the sky, a great tree, with a herdsman sitting at the foot of it. On low bank to the left, another tree, leafless and bare, with its roots in the water. A level champaign in the distance. 20½ by 32 *inches.* 52 by 81·33 *centimètres.* [1147.

Lent by ALEXANDER YOUNG, Esq., London.

17. An Evening in Normandy.

A piece of waste land, green and broken, with a group of trees receding in the distance. In the left foreground a woman gathering sticks. Grey and green, with, as it were, a general effect of gold. 17¾ by 21½ *inches.* 45 by 54·50 *centimètres.* [1126.

ETCHING. *Lent by* ONE OF THE COMMITTEE.

18. Landscape with Dog.

A lake. On the right bank a tree. In the distance, on the left, a castled promontory. In the foreground a red and white dog. 15½ by 19 *inches.* 39·50 by 48·33 *centimètres.* [1088.

Lent by ALEXANDER YOUNG, Esq., London.

19. The Hay-Cart.

A wagon and horses crossing a stream. On the right a single tree. Sunlit meadows in the distance. 12½ by 17¾ *inches.* 32 *by* 45 *centimètres.* [1164.

Lent by JAMES STAAT-FORBES, Esq., London.

20. Les Gaulois : The Road to the Camping Ground.

A road, with sandhills on the left, where is also a slim, bare tree, with, in the foreground, a single horseman. On the right a great tree sloping down over the road, and with a reclining figure at its foot. A scheme of browns, greys, and faint green. 20¾ *by* 25 *inches.* 52·75 *by* 63·50 *centimètres.* [1158.

Lent by WILLIAM THORBURN, Esq., Peebles.

GUSTAVE COURBET

1819—1877

COURBET'S father, a peasant of the Doubs, would fain have made his son a lawyer; but the lad had always loved to draw and paint, and when he left Ornans for Paris (1839) he threw himself into the study of art. At Besançon, in the Seminary, he had learned a little from one Flageolet, a pupil of David; and in Paris he passed through the studios of Steuben (1788-1856) and Hesse (1806-1879). But it was the Flemings in the Louvre who set him in the way of excellence; and it was in the direct and patient study of landscape and the figure that he grew to be a master-craftsman. "Je n'ai jamais eu," he wrote, in 1851, "d'autres maîtres en peinture que la nature et la tradition;" and though he was not averse from taking credit for more than his due, there is every reason to believe that here he told the truth.

The original ideals of Romanticism were losing their hold upon youth. The movement had entered on a second phase. It had begun in a return to nature; much new matter had been garnered in, had been treated, and had in turn begun to grow old; and there were now imminent a second return to the same source of inspiration and a fresh conquest of material for art. The tide, in fact, was setting strong for realism; and Courbet, a representative painter, both by his qualities and his defects, was swept forward on the very crest of the wave. He broke ground in 1842 with a portrait—the first of many —of himself; and at the Salon of 1850—having meanwhile bemused his brain with such dubious theories, political and aesthetic, as were in the air, and made himself a host of enemies by the insolence of his conceit, which was fated to bring him to disgrace and ruin—he made a prodigious stir with a group of portraits—his own, the *Berlioz*, the *Francis Wey*, and a fourth of the madman Jean Journet; and three great subject pictures—the *Retour de Foire*, the *Casseurs de Pierres*, and the tremendous *Enterrement d'Ornans*. In 1853 he produced *Les Baigneuses*, which Proudhon mistook for a satire on a vile and shameless *bourgeoisie*. In 1855, protesting, as the hero of a one-man show, against the great official exhibition, he took opinion by storm with his *Atelier du Peintre*, a fantastic work, which was regarded at the time as a triumph of realism, and which he himself, in the jargon he loved, described as " une allégorie réelle déterminant une phase de sept années de ma vie d'artiste." From this he passed to *Le Combat des Cerfs* in 1861, *La Remise des Chevreuils* [1866], *La Sieste* in 1869, and *La Vague* in 1870. The year after he joined the Commune; made himself conspicuous in connection with the overthrow of the Vendôme Column; and, though M. Castagnary has since acquitted him of any practical share in the foolish business of the Column, for his indulgence in these "violent delights" was visited with a heavy fine and six months in jail. He came out a broken man. His intellects were none of the strongest, and the game of revolution he had tried to play, in politics and in art, had cost him all his favour and much of his talent. His death in exile was a deliverance for the man, and for the artist the beginning of a purer renown. At the exhibition of his work, which was held in Paris five years after (1882), it was recognised that, for all his blundering and extravagance, he had painted as only a master can.

He had a strong strain of vulgarity. In Millet there were none of the bad qualities of the peasant: there were few of the good ones in Courbet. A braggart and a pedant of the first water, he was grossly addicted to low company, to beer, and to the commonest forms of notoriety; apprehensive and vigorous as it was, his intelligence was yet strangely limited; while his vanity was so robust, and his egoism so active, that they are felt as evil influences not only in his life but in his art. He had the painter's hand, the painter's eye, the painter's temperament in uncommon fulness; but his capacity of divination, his perception of the hidden sense of things, though stronger and richer than he knew, were not in proportion. He believed himself to lack imagination, and prided himself on the want; derided poetry even while he unconsciously rose to it; gibed at the wiseacres who, never having seen an angel, were yet prepared to paint one; nor ever realised that (of the two flights of fancy) it is no easier to see a Courbet than to imagine an angel. "La peinture," he was wont to say, flourishing his ten fingers, "la peinture, c'est ça." It was a stupid brag; and as regards his own work, it was untrue to an extent that, had he suspected it, would have made him furious. For he painted, not with his ten fingers only, but with his brain. He thought, not deeply it may be, but he did think, and always as a painter; and he rendered his impressions with such force, simplicity, mastery of his medium, completeness of observation, and breadth of vision and effect, as exalt his good things almost to the level of greatness.

21. L'Immensité.

A stretch of level sand and quiet sea, under a mixed, uncertain sunset sky. 23 by 31 *inches*. 58·50 by 79 *centimètres*. [1086.

Lent by CONSTANTINE A. IONIDES, Esq., London.

22. Fruit.

A plate of apples and pears on a red table-cloth. 6¾ by 14 *inches*. 17 by 35·50 *centimètres*. [1103.

Lent by ROBERT RAMSEY, Esq., Glasgow.

23. An Interior, with Apples.

Apples, pears, and a pot of primulas on a white table-cloth, with a background, on the left of dark green curtain, on the right of rich furniture. Painted in Sainte-Pélagie. 23 by 28 *inches*. 58·33 by 71 *centimètres*. [1136.

Lent by JOHN GLAS SANDEMAN, Esq., London.

CHARLES-FRANÇOIS DAUBIGNY

1817—1878

THE Daubignys were landscape painters for three generations. There was no Napoleon in the family; but neither was there a King of Rome. Edmé-François, the first of the race, was, like Corot, a pupil of Victor Bertin, and the master of the artist under consideration, the more famous Charles-François, whose example and renown were continued by his son Karl, the third of the dynasty.

Charles Daubigny was born and bred in Paris. Having to work for daily bread, he spent the first years of his career in decorating box-lids and clock-cases. At eighteen he went to Italy; he painted industriously from nature at Rome, and Florence, and Naples; and returning the next year to France, he passed through the studios of Granet (1775-1849) and Paul Delaroche (1797-1856), and entered the Salon in 1838, with a *Vue de Notre Dame et de l'Île Saint-Louis*. He practised etching, original and reproductive, with some success, and, like Meissonier and Jean Gigoux, he drew on wood for the publishers of illustrated books. But he studied nature indefatigably, he developed a personal style, and in 1848, after ten years' hard work, he won a Second Class medal with his *Environs de Château-Chinon* and his *Bords de Cornin*, while in 1853 he attained to First Class honours with the *Étang de Gylieu*. Thereafter he had but to paint as he pleased. It was felt that his art was worthy of the great school of landscape of which it was a development; and although his rivals were men of the stamp of Corot, Rousseau, Courbet, and Dupré, for a quarter of a century he continued to hold his own: with the *Vendange*, the *Écluse d'Optevoz*, the *Soir à Andressy*; the *Moulins à Dordrecht*, the *Tonnelier*, and many a graceful and pleasant masterpiece besides.

That his work is unequal in quality is but to say that, like Corot, he was successful. The artist suffers in proportion as the dealer is happy; and Daubigny was sometimes careless, and could on occasion be even feeble and tame. But his good work is very good indeed, and must be judged by a standard that falls short only of the highest. He had a great love for running water: he passed much of his time in a house-boat, *le Bottin;* and, as Mr. Hamerton has noted, for his "intimate affection," his "simple devotion," to the river of his choice, he was "rewarded by an insight into its beauty," which, to compare him for a moment with the famous Englishman who had painted the Seine before him, was entirely wanting in Turner. These qualities of "intimate affection" and "simple devotion" are characteristic of Daubigny—are what, in the analysis of his individuality, is most readily disengaged; and it is, I think, from their expression that his art derives its peculiar savour. His imagination is of a far inferior strain to Rousseau's; he has elegance, distinction, charm, but not in the supreme degree that Corot has them; he is a pleasing colourist, where Diaz is a great one; his technical accomplishment is admirable, but it would be waste of words to compare it with the *maëstria* of Courbet. But the sanity and contentment of his regard for nature, his innocent and grateful confidence, as of a happy and not too masterful or curious husband—these are his own. He is perhaps the least of the great Romantic brood; but he belongs to it, and his achievement, from however lofty a level it be considered, and by whatever canons it be tried, is as safe from oblivion as it is superior to disparagement.

---

24. The Seashore.

A stretch of dark rocks covered with weed, and dotted with figures gathering kelp. A sandy beach beyond. A rainy sky, lit at the lower edge by a yellow gleam projected upon the sea and a grassy headland to the right. The scheme is one of modulated blacks and greys, with only two notes of definite colour—the aforesaid yellow and green. 13¼ by 26 *inches.* 33·50 by 66 *centimètres.*

[1135.

Lent by ONE OF THE COMMITTEE.

25. Coast Scene.

A picture of the Thames. The mouth of a river, flat-shored, with barges, boats, and topsail schooners coming up with the tide. 15¼ by 25¾ inches. 39·50 by 65·50 centimètres. [1130.

Lent by DANIEL COTTIER, Esq., London.

26. Town and River.

A river, with a bridge in the middle distance; on the right bank, in the foreground, trees, and on the left bank a city and cathedral. 8¾ by 16½ inches. 22 by 42 centimètres. [1081.

Lent by JAMES STAAT-FORBES, Esq., London.

FRENCH PICTURES

27. **Landscape : River and Cows.**

Under a grey sky, a brook flowing from the right middle distance to the left foreground, with a green meadow on the near side, and on the far a russet hillock and trees. *33 by 58¾ inches. 84 by 1 mètre 49 centimètres.* [1119.

Lent by ALEXANDER YOUNG, Esq., London.

28. **Landscape.**

A village at evening. From the right a screen of trees slopes to a river, with cattle drinking. *8 by 13¾ inches. 20·33 by 34·50 centimètres* [1095.

Lent by ROBERT STEWART, Esq., Ratho.

29. **The Stork's Retreat.**

A river at sunset, flowing between tall trees, and under a rosy sky, with a stork wading. *7½ by 11 inches. 19 by 28 centimètres.* [1163.

Lent by JAMES STAAT-FORBES, Esq., London.

30. Moonlight.

A summer moonlight on a still river. On the left a bank, with trees reflected in the water; a low bank on the right; a file of ducks crossing the stream. 15½ by 25¼ inches. 39·50 by 64·50 *centimètres*. [1175.

Lent by JAMES STAAT-FORBES, Esq., London.

31. Sun Setting over the Sea.

A grey sky with tawny clouds, in the extreme right of which the sun is sinking, like a scarlet ball, into an expanse of rough and sullen blue sea, deserted save for a single fishing-boat. 20½ by 36½ inches. 52 by 93 *centimètres*. [1074.

Lent by the Hon. Mr. JUSTICE DAY, London.

32. Landscape.

A sketch from nature. Under a cloudy, grey sky, a green field sloping down from the right to a wall lined with trees; on the left a piece of rising ground. 19½ by 31½ inches. 49·50 by 80 *centimètres*. [1155.

Lent by ALEXANDER BOWMAN, Esq., Edinburgh.

33. Landscape.

A river, green with weeds, flows into the picture. On the right a grassy bank, with black cattle coming down to drink. 16 by 26¼ *inches.* 40·50 by 67·50 *centimètres.* [1160.

Lent by ALEXANDER YOUNG, Esq., London.

34. Landscape.

A river green with weeds, and dotted with a file of ducks. A cluster of trees on the right bank, under a pink sky. Sketch of an effect in pink and green. 14½ by 26¼ *inches.* 37 by 66·50 *centimètres.* [1089.

Lent by JAMES DONALD, Esq., Glasgow.

35. Landscape with Lake.

Green meadows and winding water; with trees and cattle. A summer pastoral. 13 by 22¼ *inches.* 33 by 56·50 *centimètres.* [1073.

Lent by JAMES STAAT-FORBES, Esq., London.

36. Landscape.

A river flowing in from the right foreground, with a low wood on the far bank. On the left the near bank, with a road and a fleet of boats moored inshore, and in the background a plantation. 15 by 26 *inches.* 38 by 66 *centimètres.* [1167.

Lent by ALEXANDER YOUNG, Esq., London.

ALEXANDRE-GABRIEL DECAMPS

1803—1860

LTHOUGH born in Paris, Gabriel Decamps spent much of his childhood in Picardy, associating on equal terms with peasant boys and girls, sharing in their sports and broils, and running wild with the wildest. The training was in some ways bad, for it made him idle and intolerant of the yoke. On the other hand, it taught him to know the aspects and the ways of horses and dogs and cattle; it encouraged a natural predilection for adventure; it made him a traveller; it kept him unconventional and the enemy of what is merely commonplace and dull; and thus it may fairly be said to have been good.

Returning to the capital, he worked, according to his humour, in this studio and in that—now with Bouchod (1800-1842), now with Abel de Pujol (1785-1861); and after trying his hand in *genre* and animal painting, he went off on a *Wanderjahr*, in the course of which he saw not only Italy and Switzerland, but the cities of the Levant as well. For these latter he did what Delacroix was presently to do for Morocco and Algiers; he took possession of them in the name of art, and, though he rendered what he saw with little care for nature, he opened up to the painters of his time and ours a new province of material. Among his trophies were the *Patrouille Turque* (1827), the *Corps de Garde* (1834), and the *École Turque* (1847). Such success, however, was not enough for his ambition. He aspired to paint religion and history, as well as Smyrniote life and true Levantine light and colour; and in 1834, when he exhibited his famous *Défaite des Cimbres*, he had his hour of triumph. It was his one great success in this department—he never reached again the same degree of popularity. And the reasons are not far to seek. For one thing, Romanticism was not officially accepted: it was understood to mean no more than immorality in theory, and incompetence in practice; and Decamps was one of the ensigns of Romanticism. For another, his education was imperfect, his brain and hand were out of unison; the one might plan, but the other could not execute. Decamps was naturally proud and angry; and it is not surprising that he should soon have chosen to avoid the trials and disasters of publicity. After 1834 he exhibited but seldom, sold his pictures straight from the easel, and spent his life in profitless attempts at heroic work. "You are a lucky fellow," he said to Millet, after the painter of *Le Semeur* had shown him all the pictures in his studio, "you can do what you want to do." Decamps could not; and he died (of a fall from his horse) a disappointed man.

He was hardly one of the paladins of Romanticism; but he bore no inconspicuous part in the battle, and his influence was good in type and considerable in degree. His intelligence—quick, inquiring, tenacious—readily received new truths and new ideas; he was the sworn admirer of such great explorers as Rousseau and Delacroix; of its kind his interest in nature was both vigorous and sustained; as a colourist he was individual enough to have had many imitators; he grappled hard with the problems of illumination and atmospheric environment; and as a pioneer and experimentalist he is deserving of much respect. He lived to witness the triumph of Romanticism; but the greater honours and rewards of victory were not for him, and it is perhaps as the discoverer of the painters' East that he will be best remembered.

37. A Stable.

A stable with three horses, and a groom pouring corn from a bag into a sieve. 21¼ by 18¼ *inches.* 54 by 46·33 *centimètres.* [1127]

Lent by PERCY WESTMACOTT, Esq., Newcastle-on-Tyne.

FERDINAND-VICTOR-EUGÈNE
DELACROIX

1799—1863

HARLES-CONSTANT DELACROIX, born in Champagne (1740), played many parts, and played them well. He began life as an advocate, was Turgot's secretary, represented the Department of the Marne in the National Convention, was Foreign Secretary, and then Ambassador to Holland, under the Directorate, and, finally, was made Prefect, first of the Bouches-du-Rhône, and afterwards of the Gironde, during his tenure of which last office he died (1805) at Bordeaux. His wife, Victoire Oeben, was a daughter of a famous *ébéniste* (a pupil of Boulle) and a certain Françoise Vandercreuse, whose second husband was the illustrious Riesener. Of their four children, the eldest, Charles-Henri, served Napoleon with distinction, and died a general, a Commander of the Legion of Honour, and a Baron of the Empire; the second, whose portrait is esteemed one of the masterpieces of David, was the wife of M. de Verninac Saint-Maur, sometime Ambassador at Constantinople; Henri, the third, was killed at Friedland; and the youngest, Ferdinand-Victor-Eugène, was the most famous painter of his generation, and is now acclaimed by his countrymen for the greatest of the century.

He was educated in Paris, at the Lycée Louis-le-Grand, where, says a class-mate, Philarète Chasles, at eight or nine years old, "il couvrait ses cahiers de dessins et de bonshommes," in which he "reproduisait les attitudes, inventait les raccourcis, dessinait et variait tous les costumes, poursuivant, torturant, multipliant la forme sous tous les aspects avec une obstination semblable à la fureur." Something he learned from his uncle Riesener, the miniature and portrait painter (1767-1828); and in 1815, having lost his fortune and both his parents, and despairing of advancement under the Bourbons, he entered the studio of Guérin (1774-1833). Here he worked at the antique and the figure with that feverish tenacity which was one of his characteristics; here he was still a student when in 1822 he exhibited his *Dante et Virgile*, and conquered reputation at a stroke. Gros (1771-1835), who described the picture as "du Rubens châtié," offered to receive him into his studio; but Delacroix, much as he admired that master, refused the honourable opportunity, and remained with Guérin, though Guérin cared nothing for his work, until the end. The young man had something to say, and was bent on saying it in terms of his own; he was, besides, a great believer in gymnastics—all his life long he never sat down to paint without making a sketch from Poussin, or Raphael, or the antique; and it is probable he thought Guérin, who was only a good sound academical draughtsman, a better master than Gros, whose manner was more personal, and whose talent had certain analogies with his own. For the plastic and decorative parts of art, he studied these elsewhere: in the studios of Géricault (1791-1824), and Bonington (1801-1828), and Paul Huet (1804-1869); in the Louvre under the influence of Rubens; in the Jardin des Plantes with Barye (1795-1875). His indebtedness to Constable (1776-1837), under whose inspiration he completely repainted his second great picture, the *Massacre de Scio*, is matter of history; but it is fair to add that he is said to have anticipated that master's innovations in landscape studies of his own doing, before *The Hay Wain* appeared upon the scene. In 1825 he went to England (Bonington and Isabey were of the party), where he knew Lawrence and Wilkie, heard the *Freischütz* ("avec de la musique qu'on a supprimée à Paris"), was subjugated by the genius of Shakespeare and Kean, and impelled anew in the direction of nature and romance. In 1826-27 he produced, among other things, the famous lithographs in illustration of *Faust*, in which Goethe declared him to have surpassed the author's own conceptions. In 1828 he exhibited the *Mort de Sardanapale*, the *Christ au Jardin des Oliviers*, and the *Marino Faliero*; and in 1830 he painted the inspired *Le Vingt-Huit Juillet*. Two years afterwards he went to Morocco (with the Ambassador, M. de Mornay) and to Algiers, and brought back the material for the *Femmes d'Alger*, the *Convulsionnaires de Tanger*, the

Noce Juïve, and other masterpieces in the same vein. It was the last but one of his journeys. Italy he never saw. He made the round of the Belgian galleries in 1838; and thereafter he quitted France no more.

From the first (much against his will, for he was a nervous and febrile creature, elegant in manner, refined in taste, incapable of pose, and intolerant of notoriety) he had been saluted as a champion of Romanticism. But he had seen such mediocrities as Louis Boulanger and Eugène Devéria preferred to him in the past; and it was not until the Salon of 1833 had revealed him for a master· that he took his place in the forefront of the movement as the equal of Hugo in verse and of Dumas in drama, as a captain of the revolutionary army. Then came the *Bataille de Taillebourg gagnée par Saint Louis*, the *Barque de Don Juan*, the *Bataille de Nancy*, the *Combat du Giaour et du Pacha*, the *Boissy d'Anglas*, the *Ovide chez les Scythes*, the *Justice de Trajan*, the *Médée*, the *Muley Abd-el-Rahman*, the *Entrée des Croisés à Constantinople*, the decorations of the Palais-Bourbon, the Louvre, the Hôtel de Ville, the *Héliodore* and the *Lutte de Jacob avec l'Ange* at Saint-Sulpice—a world of moving and intense creation; and still his success was only partial. Though Couture affected to despise him, and to Ingres and his followers he was anathema, the painters were with him almost to a man; Courbet himself, though he assumed he could do as well or better—even Courbet is found admitting the superiority of the *Massacre de Scio*. But the public were interested in other things—the plaintive heroics of Ary Scheffer, the "last tableaux" of Delaroche. The *Hamlet* of 1836 was very far from being the only work of his rejected by the jury; to the anger and amazement of Théodore Rousseau, the *Croisés à Constantinople* itself was coldly received, and it was only in 1855 that the painter's force was fully recognised. In 1859, after several repulses, and the preference (amongst others) of Schnetz and Cogniet, he was elected a Member of the Institute, and exhibited for the last time; and four years after, he died. His greatest triumph was yet to come. The exhibition of the pictures and drawings found in his studio was, says M. Burty, "une réhabilitation et une ivresse." Art was far cheaper then than now; but instead of the hundred thousand francs at which these relics had been appraised, nearly three and a half times that amount was realised by the sale. Millet, whose fortunes were at their lowest ebb, was among the buyers; it was hard work for him to get daily bread, but he could not deny himself a Delacroix drawing.

Apart from his art, Delacroix was a man of singular intelligence, lettered, of a trenchant insight and broad sympathies. In music his idols were Beethoven and Mozart; he had no liking for the innovations of Berlioz, and could not endure his own to be compared with them. His essays and sketches are something more than good reading; they prove that in painting his tastes were not less catholic than sound. He accepted Raphael and Poussin as completely as Rubens and Rembrandt; he thought the world of Charlet, and the world of Ingres likewise; he reverenced Holbein, but that did not prevent him from greatly admiring Géricault and Lawrence; his criticisms, in a word, are those of a painter who has mastered the theory as well as the practice of his art, and is alive to beauty in any and every form. For his place in art, it has yet to be decided. In France, as I have said, he is a national glory; in England, where he is little known, and where he is considered with a certain jealousy, as one who compelled success in a department of painting where certain Englishmen had found nothing but disaster, his technical accomplishment has been denied, and his inspiration dismissed as factitious, even vulgar. It is argued that he was too thoroughly a Frenchman of 1830 to be interesting to all time and to all peoples; and in the argument there is no doubt a certain truth, as there is in its converse, that it is precisely because he was a typical Frenchman and a representative of his epoch that he is to be accepted now as the greatest artist of his century. It will probably be found that the final judgment will contain something of both these. What Delacroix did was to express the spirit, the tendencies, the ideals, the passions, the weaknesses of a new age in terms so novel and forcible as to be absolutely appropriate. The violence, the brutality, the insincerity, the bad taste, of which it is complained, were not specially his: they were inherent in the movement, and we must allow for them in Delacroix as we allow for them in Byron and Hugo, in *Atala* and the *Symphonie Fantastique*, in *Antony* and *Rolla* and *La Peau de Chagrin*. It is safe to say that, if that be done, much will remain that is imperishable. It has yet to be proved that his literary imagination—the gift of evocation which made him the familiar and the commentator of Ariosto, Dante, Shakespeare, Scott, Byron, and Goethe: the quality, says Baudelaire, "qui fait de lui le peintre aimé des poètes"—is human and sound enough to survive the touch of time. Of his plastic endowment there can be no such doubt. If he was nothing else he was a painter, and if he did nothing else he thought in pictures. His colour—though Rossetti did not like it—is not the dress, the decoration, of his ideas, but a vital part of them; often loose and incorrect, his drawing is always expressive and significant; his invention is inexhaustible; his capacity of treatment may be compared with that of Hugo in words and with that of Berlioz in music. There is no department of painting in which he did not try his hand, and none on which he did not leave his mark. History and romance, religion and portraiture, *genre* and landscape and the figure—in all of them he was Eugène Delacroix.

"En le supprimant," says Baudelaire, "on supprimerait un monde de sensations et d'idées, on ferait une lacune trop grande dans la chaîne historique." That is the poet's view. The painter is not less imperious and explicit. "Nous ne sommes plus au temps des Olympiens," says Théodore Rousseau, "comme Raphaël, Veronèse, et Rubens, et l'art de Delacroix"—that Delacroix who "représente l'esprit, le verbe de son temps," and in whose "lamentations exagérées" and whose "triomphes retentissants" there is always "le souffle de la poitrine, son cri, son mal, et le nôtre"—that art is "puissant comme une voix de l'enfer du Dante." Here is a curiosity of art criticism: perhaps for the only time in history, the poetic and the technical critic are at one.

38. After Rubens.

A free and very personal study of *Le Gouvernement de la Reine*, one of the cartoons designed by Rubens for the decoration of the Luxembourg. The original, which is described at length in the official catalogue of the Louvre, *Écoles Allemande, Flamande et Hollandaise*, No. 445, measures 3·94 mètres by 7·02 mètres. 19¼ *by* 12 *inches*. 49·50 *by* 30·50 *centimètres*. [1111.

Lent by DANIEL COTTIER, Esq., London.

39. The Good Samaritan.

A road with trees. To the left the traveller fallen among thieves; bending above him from the right, in a crimson cloak, the Samaritan. In the background, cropping the grass, the Samaritan's ass. A scheme of brown and crimson. 12¼ *by* 15½ *inches*. 31 *by* 39·50 *centimètres*. [1143.

Lent by CONSTANTINE A. IONIDES, Esq., London.

40. La Barque de Don Juan.

The sketch for the picture in the Louvre. The foreground is occupied by a boat seen broadside on, which is crowded with figures. All the rest is dark sky and sullen and oily green sea, with, on the right, the red disc of the half-sunken sun. 31¼ by 38¾ inches. 79·33 by 98·50 centimètres. [1098.

Lent by CONSTANTINE A. IONIDES, Esq., London.

NARCISSE-VIRGILIO DIAZ DE LA PEÑA

1808—1876

THE painter of the *Nymphe Endormie* and the *Fin d'un Beau Jour*—"the Anacreon of the Bas-Bréau"—was a Frenchman only by accident. His father and mother, Tomas Diaz and Maria Velasco, were Spaniards of Salamanca, driven into exile by the failure of a conspiracy against King Joseph Bonaparte. Their child was born in Bordeaux; while the father, exiled from France, as well as from his native country, betook himself, alone, to Norway, and passing thence to London, died in that city, just as his wife was on the point of setting sail from the Gironde to join him. Being utterly friendless, she came north, to Paris first, and then to Sèvres, where she supported herself and her child by giving lessons in Spanish and Italian. At the latter place she died, and Narcisse-Virgilio, now a boy of ten, was adopted by the Protestant pastor of Bellevue, with whom he remained until he came to Paris to seek his fortune.

When he was fifteen he got stung in the left foot by a poison-fly (he was to die of a snake-bite more than half a century after), and twice he had to suffer amputation. But his energy, of mind and body alike, was extraordinary, and he went on riding and dancing and swimming as before. Being called upon to choose a trade, he took—like Raffet and Jules Dupré—to china-painting. But, whenever he could, he engaged himself in oils as well. He worked under Souchon (1787-1857); and in 1831 he got his first picture into the Salon. At this time, and for some years, he was only as it were an understudy of Delacroix. He painted flowers, battles, portraits, naked women, anything that would sell (it is on record that for some of these works he was content to take as little as five francs apiece); and even his colour —in after years so rich, so distinguished, so eminently personal — was imitated from his leader's. At forty he was still learning to draw; but so early as 1836-37 he had fallen under the inspiring influence of Rousseau, and was on the way to become the great artificer in sunshine and leafage that we know.

For a dozen years or so he exhibited rather unsuccessfully than not. But in 1844 he won a Third Class medal with a *Bas-Bréau*, an *Orientale*, and a *Bohémiens se rendant à une Fête*; in 1846, a Second Class, with the *Délaissées*, the *Magicienne*, the *Jardin des Amours*, an *Intérieur de Forêt*, a *Léda*; and in 1848, a First Class, with a *Diane partant pour la Chasse*, a *Meute dans la Forêt de Fontainebleau*, a *Vénus et Adonis*; while in 1851 he exhibited a portrait, a *Baigneuse*, and his *Amour Désarmé*, and received the ribbon of the Legion of Honour. Henceforward life was easy enough; and though in 1855 he failed with his most ambitious work—the much-debated and much-ridiculed *Dernières Larmes*—he succeeded splendidly with half-a-dozen others : the *Rivales*, the *Nymphe tourmentée par l'Amour*, the *Fin d'un Beau Jour*, among them. His last Salon was that of 1859; but if he abstained from exhibiting he nowise ceased from production. In 1860 he lost his son Émile, a painter like himself and like himself a pupil of Rousseau; but not even that great affliction could break his spirit or abate his interest in art. There were fifteen years of life before him still—"railleur, mais non amer, spirituel, parfois un peu brusque, au fond *bon et franc comme du pain de froment*"— and fifteen years of work. To the end he lived but to paint; and, as we have seen, his death, at sixty-eight, was a result of accident. Millet and Corot had passed the year before; and when he followed them, of the great and famous group to which we owe the best of modern art only Dupré and Daubigny were left alive.

Diaz had many masters—Delacroix, Correggio, Millet, Rousseau, Prud'hon —and succumbed to many influences in turn. But if he followed, it was only that he might learn to lead; if he copied, it was the more completely to express himself. His master qualities are fancy and charm; but capricious as he was, and enchanting as he never failed to be, he was a devout student and a rare observer of nature. "Personne," says M. Jules Dupré, "n'a compris mieux que lui la loi de la lumière, la magie, et pour ainsi dire la

folie, du soleil dans les feuilles et les sous-bois." What gives his work its peculiar quality of delightfulness is the combination of lovely fact with graceful fiction. His world would be Arcadia if it were not so real—would be the world we live in if it did not teem with exquisite impossibilities. I think of him as of an amiable and light-hearted Rembrandt. He had a touch of the madness of genius, or that madness of the sunshine (of which his old companion speaks) would certainly have escaped him. And rightly to express his ideas and sensations, he made himself a wonderful vocabulary. His palette was composed, not of common pigments, but of molten jewels; they clash in the richest chords, they sing in triumphant unisons, as do the elements of music in a score of Berlioz. If they meant nothing they would still be delicious. But beyond them is Diaz—the poet, the *fantaisiste*, the artist; and that makes them unique.

---

41. Landscape : Evening.

A piece of broken ground, with a pool in which are reflected the form and colour of the sunset sky above. To the left a leafy tree, with a man fishing. In the background a stretch of landscape with a farm. 14¼ *by* 21 *inches*. 36 *by* 53·50 *centimètres*. [1072.

Lent by ALEXANDER YOUNG, Esq., London.

42. Landscape.

On the right, against a soft, cloudy sky, a hill with grey rocks and, beyond, a space of undulating distance. An impression of warm, suffused sunlight. 8½ *by* 15½ *inches*. 21·50 *by* 39·50 *centimètres*. [1077.

Lent by DANIEL COTTIER, Esq., London.

43. Sunset : Autumn.

In the foreground a pool, with a woman seated hard by. To the left a tall brown poplar reared against a luminous sunset sky, the light of which floods a mass of forest in the background, and is reverberated from a touch of brilliant scarlet in the figure's cap. 17½ *by* 11 *inches*. 44·50 *by* 28 *centimètres*. [1123.

ETCHING. *Lent by* ONE OF THE COMMITTEE.

44. A Wood-Nymph.

The interior of a wood, in which is seated a naked nymph not unsuggestive of Correggio. 12½ by 9½ inches. 32 by 24 centimètres. [1117.

Lent by PERCY WESTMACOTT, Esq., Newcastle-on-Tyne.

45. The Chase.

A forest path, with a pack of hounds in full cry. In the distance a landscape of wood and hill, with an effect of late sunset. A scheme of sumptuous autumnal colouring. 13½ by 9 inches. 34·33 by 23 centimètres. [1118.

Lent by DANIEL COTTIER, Esq., London.

46. The Edge of the Forest.

Under a stormy sky a broken road in the open forest. In the left foreground a single tree; a group in the middle distance to the right. In the centre foreground a woman in a red petticoat. 10½ by 13½ inches. 26·50 by 34·50 centimètres.
[1151.

Lent by ONE OF THE COMMITTEE.

47. The Bather.

A rocky glade (Fontainebleau), with a bathing nymph in the centre. A scheme of cool grey, green, and blue. 9½ by 12¾ inches. 24 by 32·50 centimètres.
[1142.

Lent by CONSTANTINE A. IONIDES, Esq., London.

48. The Forest.

Leading into the picture, a sandy track, under oak trees—a *sous-bois*, in fact—filled with sunshine. 12½ by 17 inches. 32 by 43·33 centimètres. [1096.

Lent by JAMES STAAT-FORBES, Esq., London.

49. Flowers.

> An oval panel filled, chiefly, with red roses and peonies. 24 by 19½ inches. 61 by 49·50 centimètres. [1128.
>
> *Lent by* Mrs. JOHN ELDER, Glasgow.

50. 'Autumn.'

> A life-size allegorical figure, with fruit, the flesh-tints contrasted with, and relieved against, a drapery of Titianic blue. In the background a conventional landscape. A decorative panel, painted to be seen from a certain distance. 85 by 56 inches. 2 mètres 16 centimètres by 1 mètre 42 centimètres. [1133.
>
> *Lent by* JAMES INGLIS, Esq., New York.

51. Flowers.

> A decorative oval, the companion to . 24 by 19 inches. by 48·33 centimètres. [1139.
>
> *Lent by* JAMES STAAT-FORBES, Esq., London.

52. Landscape.

> A rocky waste, with trees, lit by a gleam of sunshine from a stormy sky. 9 by 12¼ inches. 23 by 31·75 centimètres. [1149.
>
> *Lent by* JAMES STAAT-FORBES, Esq., London.

53. Woodland Landscape.

> View down a forest path, with tall, rich-tinted, autumnal trees on either hand. 16¾ by 13 inches. 42·50 by 33 centimètres. [1153.
>
> *Lent by* ONE OF THE COMMITTEE.

54. Landscape : Evening.

> The heart of an oak wood with sunshine glistening through the leafage. In the foreground, a woman gathering sticks. 6¼ by 10 inches. 15·75 by 25·50 centimètres. [1162.
>
> *Lent by* CONSTANTINE A. IONIDES, Esq., London.

JULES DUPRÉ

BORN AT NANTES, 1811

THE father of M. Dupré was a potter, and the son began by painting china, with Cabat and Raffet, in Paris. From this he passed to the studio of the younger Diébold (born 1779); and in 1831 broke ground as a landscape painter with five *Paysages* from Montmorency, L'Isle-Adam, and the valley of the Vienne. He succeeded at once; and in 1833 he received a Second Class medal for an *Intérieur de Ferme*. But he soon became disgusted with publicity, and for many years he has painted for himself alone. In 1849 he won the red ribbon; to the Great Exhibition of 1867 he sent a dozen pictures, and was rewarded with another Second Class medal; and since then he has exhibited but once, at the Salon Triennal of 1883. The fact is, he is an artist who cares nothing for money or fame and everything for art; he is able to follow his bent, and paint as he pleases, and he has had his reward. To the young zealots who have just discovered the Blue Shadow his name and example are of small account. But by artists he is respected and acclaimed as the last of a greater generation.

He is still a contemporary; and to estimate the worth of his art is impossible. It may, however, be said that his achievement is both vast and varied, and is touched throughout with a peculiar poetry. As becomes the friend and champion of Rousseau, the great experimentalist, the indefatigable explorer, he has attempted nature in all its aspects. He has painted the melancholy of the plain, the peaceful serenity of fat pasture and pleasant upland, the mystery of the forest, the greatness of the sea; and he has infused with his own sincere personality whatever he has done. In an age of backsliding and charlatanism he has upheld the dignity of imaginative art, and the traditions of the school he helped to found and has done so much to illustrate.

55. Sea with Boat.

A green-grey sea and sky, with a dark brown smack running, close-reefed, before the gale. 21½ by 17¾ inches. 54·50 by 45 centimètres. [1070.

Lent by THE HON. MR. JUSTICE DAY, London.

56. Pointe des Dunes.

A rocky point, with a breaking wave to the right. The rest is green-blue sea and sky, with an impression, nearer home, of brown herbage. 28¼ by 36 inches. 71·33 by 91·50 centimètres. [1099.

ETCHING. *Lent by* JAMES DONALD, Esq., Glasgow.

57. Marine.

A waste of green-blue sea and sky, with a smack in a gale of wind. 13½ by 10⅜ inches. 34·33 by 26·50 centimètres. [1104.

Lent by ANDREW J. KIRKPATRICK, Esq., Glasgow.

58. Landscape with Cattle.

A stream, with cattle wading, in an open park. 8 by 10½ inches. 20·33 by 26·75 centimètres. [1166.

Lent by JAMES STAAT-FORBES, Esq., London.

59. Boat at Sea.

A brown-sailed smack, crossing the line of a clouded sunset. 14⅜ by 18 *inches.*
37·50 by 46 *centimètres.* [1121.

Lent by JAMES STAAT-FORBES, Esq., London.

IGNAZ-HENRI-JEAN-THÉODORE
FANTIN-LATOUR

Born at Grenoble, 1836

STUDYING under his father, a good artist in pastels, Fantin-Latour, like so many of his generation—MM. Cazin, Legros, Guillaume Regamey, and Auguste Rodin among them—became for some time a pupil of Lecoq de Boisbaudran. After this he passed through the École des Beaux-Arts, and worked a while with Courbet; and in 1861 he was seen for the first time in the Salon. Since then he has exhibited many essays in allegory, still-life, portraiture; he has achieved considerable success in pastel and lithography; he was decorated in 1878, after winning Third and Second Class medals in 1870-72. Among the more important of his works are the *Hommage à Delacroix* (1863), the *Toast* (1865), the *Atelier à Batignolles* and the *Coin de Table* (1872), the *Famille D——* (1878), the *Autour du Piano* (1884), all experiments in portraiture; the allegorical *Anniversaire de Berlioz* (1876): and the fourteen lithographs done for the *Richard Wagner* (1886) of M. Adolphe Jullien. In England he is best known as a painter of flowers.

His art is a development of Romanticism. His portrait groups are modern in every sense of the word; his allegorical pictures have a certain smack of 1830 and of the Courbet of the *Atelier du Peintre*; he is a student of atmosphere and light, and has recorded his impressions in appropriate and novel terms. Of late years his manner has become a little hard and dry, and his care for detail somewhat exaggerated. But he is always a craftsman, and in his best work he is a genuine colourist and something of a poet.

60. **Female Figures.**

A Muse crowning a poet. In the foreground a woman with a lyre. 12½ by 9½ inches. 32 by 24 centimètres. [1101.

Lent by ARTHUR SANDERSON, Esq., Glasgow.

61. **Dahlias.**

A bunch of dahlias in a glass. 11¼ by 14½ inches. 28·50 by 37 centimètres. [1110.

Lent by ONE OF THE COMMITTEE.

62. Erigone.

In the foreground, under a tree, the naked figure of the nymph. A distant landscape of trees, lake, and hill. 7¾ by 14¾ *inches.* 19·50 by 37·50 *centimètres.*
[1100.

Lent by ONE OF THE COMMITTEE.

63. The Bather.

A half-length female figure, naked against a background of foliage. 9 by 6¼ *inches.* 23 by 15·50 *centimètres.* [1172.

Lent by JOHN A. CAMPBELL, Esq., Glasgow.

64. Hercules between Virtue and Vice.

The demi-god in blue, two allegorical figures in white, and two others, one in white and one in red. In the background a blue-green landscape. 9¼ by 11½ *inches.* 23·50 by 29 *centimètres.* [1112.

Lent by ALEXANDER BOWMAN, Esq., Edinburgh.

65. The Bathers.

A grassy bank overlooking the sea, with two naked figures, one seated, the other standing. 6 by 9½ *inches.* 15·33 by 24 *centimètres.* [1165.

Lent by ALEXANDER BOWMAN, Esq., Edinburgh.

66. Female Figure.

In a setting of foliage a woman partially draped in red, half-seated and half-reclined, her right arm raised. 7½ by 5¾ *inches.* 19 by 14·50 *centimètres.*
[1174.

Lent by ONE OF THE COMMITTEE.

ÉDOUARD FRERE

1819—1886

ARIS was the birthplace of Édouard Frère. He was a pupil of Paul Delaroche, and, as a student at the École des Beaux-Arts, exhibited as early as 1842; but had to draw on wood for a living, and only began to emerge from obscurity in 1848, when he showed the *Petit Saltimbanque*, the *Plagiaire*, and the *Poule aux Œufs d'Or*.
Medalled in 1851 and 1852, he was decorated in 1855; he was discovered by Mr. Ruskin, who compared his colour with Rembrandt's, and remarked (if I remember aright) that he "painted with his soul," and combined "the depth of Wordsworth, the grace of Reynolds, and the holiness of Angelico"; he sold himself for twenty years to a Brussels dealer. In a word, he made his fortune, and, applauded everywhere, was especially successful in England and the United States. The list of his pictures, which have been reproduced by every sort of process, is long.

He is in every sense of the term a popular artist. His talent—originally simple, pleasing, sincere—but ill withstood the influence of the enterprising dealer and the unenlightened buyer. It is easy enough to "wallow in the pathetic"; and, as Frère discovered, it is not less profitable than it is easy. On the other hand, his good work is quite good of its kind. Mr. Ruskin's enthusiasm is not in these days easy to understand; and the question whether Frère did or did not "paint with his soul" has ceased to have any special interest. But there is no doubt that he had character, expression, a certain grace, a genuine vein of feeling. In the beginning, too, he painted much from nature, and showed himself by no means indifferent to the practice of his great contemporaries. Perhaps the worst that can be said of him is that, a sentimentalist himself, he exaggerated his defects for the pleasure of a sentimental public; but that, if it be true, is bad enough to be a lasting reproach.

67. Children in Fields.

Three girls in a sunlit meadow, with outhouses beyond, and an autumn-tinted orchard. 13 *by* 10 *inches*. 33 *by* 25·50 *centimètres*. [1122.

Lent by JAMES STAAT-FORBES, Esq., London.

JEAN-AUGUSTE-DOMINIQUE INGRES

1780—1867

IKE father, like son. Joseph Ingres, the "ornemaniste" of Montauban, was as it were an anticipation-in-little of the painter of the *Bertin* and the *Saint Symphorien*. Architect, sculptor, painter, musician, a disciple of the classic in art as it was understood and practised in the latter half of the Eighteenth Century, he handed down this intellectual estate to his son and pupil. The classic influence, indeed, was in the air. Ingres was born into an epoch which tempered revolt and massacre with a studied mimicry of the antique; and when, after a term of work at Toulouse, under Roques (1754-1847), who had been the friend and fellow-student of Louis David at Rome, under Vien (1716-1809), he came to Paris, and was received (1796) in David's studio—"David," said he, "a été le seul maître de notre siècle"—he was already himself. Already, that is, he considered form to be the great essential in art, and saw in painting not colour or handling, but only drawing and design.

Under David, "a sculptor in two dimensions," these tendencies were steadily developed. In 1801 he gained the Prix de Rome; but the State had no money to spare, and it was not until 1806 that he could take his place in the Villa Médicis, where he remained some fourteen years, addicting himself, like his master, to the study of the paintings of Herculaneum and Pompeii, and, unlike him, to the worship of Raphael, whose work he pored over, analysed, and copied with all the force of an ardent and resolute nature. During this period, too, he painted for himself with amazing industry. His exhibits included the *Œdipe et le Sphinx* and the *Odalisque*; in some others he anticipated the material of Romanticism. But it was only in 1824 that his *Vœu de Louis Treize* made him suddenly famous. Hitherto the classics had disdained him ; but he now took his place at the head of the anti-revolutionary army, and for the next ten years he combated upon their side. He had many pupils, and his authority, immense as it was, was increased from time to time by the production of such master-works as the *Bertin*, the *Apothéose d'Homère*, the *Martyre de Saint Symphorien*. In 1834 he left once more for Rome, this time as Director of the Villa Médicis; and during his tenure of office, which ended in 1841, he produced the *Stratonice*, the *Vierge à l'Hostie*, and the *Cherubini*. For the rest of his life he made his home in Paris, where, till the end, he drew, painted, and taught with admirable energy and perseverance, and a devotion to the principles of art, as he understood them, which resembled the enthusiasm of religion.

Ingres was rude, quarrelsome, violent, excessive in his likes and dislikes. He openly insulted Delacroix—"Monsieur, le dessin est la probité de l'art" —who was one of the staunchest and the most intelligent of his admirers; he was intolerant of all the works and ways of Romanticism; he called Rubens "the genius of evil," and held that to compare "Rembrandt and the others" with "the divine Raphael" and the Italians was simple blasphemy. But his sincerity was such, and such were his talent and accomplishment, that where he did not excite enthusiasm he commanded respect. Romanticism is already ancient history ; but the fame of Ingres has suffered little change, and even in the anarchy of to-day, when Delacroix is voted dull, and Corot is superannuate, and even Millet and Rousseau are Old Masters in the bad sense of the term, his work is found admirable by painters of all schools alike. The reason seems to be that what he did was undeniably well done. His colour is cold and thin ; such feeling as he had for the medium of paint was not innate but acquired ; and his convention, received from David, and improved after the Raphael of the *Stanze*, is not real enough to be human or lofty enough to be heroic. But in its way his draughtsmanship is almost impeccable ; and if it be true that he considered painting as less a special art than a development of sculpture, it is also true that in the application of this theory he has not often been excelled.

68. L'Odalisque.

A variation on one of the painter's favourite themes. A naked girl asleep on a pile of red cushions, in an attitude at once learned in arrangement and startling in effect. 11¼ *by* 18½ *inches.* 28·50 *by* 47 *centimètres.* [1173.

Lent by CONSTANTINE A. IONIDES, Esq., London.

CHARLES JACQUE

BORN AT PARIS, 1813

HARLES JACQUE began life in a lawyer's office, where, to amuse himself, he copied lithographs. Then he enlisted in the line, and was a soldier for five years, during which time he made drawings, and sold them for a franc apiece. In 1836 he came to England, and worked there for the wood-engravers, among other things, upon an illustrated *Shakespeare* and a new *Dance of Death*. Returning to Paris, after a stay in London of close on two years, he helped to embellish a famous edition of *Paul et Virginie*, a *Béranger*, a *Perrault*, a *Bretagne Illustrée*, and began to produce himself in etching. It was not until 1845 that he started work in oils and appeared, some years ahead of Millet, as a painter of rustic subjects, which, unlike his successor's, were mostly taken from the henhouse and the fold. He was Millet's neighbour at Barbizon for many years; with that painter, indeed, and with Théodore Rousseau, he may be said to have composed the famous "École de Fontainebleau." I shall have said enough if I add that in 1858 he published a treatise, illustrated by himself, of the art and mystery of keeping fowls; that, as painter and as etcher, he has been the recipient of as many as seven Third Class medals; that in 1867 he was admitted into the Legion of Honour; that he does not often exhibit; and that since he became illustrious the market has been flooded with forgeries of his work.

He and Troyon are the *animaliers* of the modern school of landscape. He has etched and painted sheep and pigs and fowls as few have done; and if his fame be not the highest it is yet high enough. His sheepfolds have little in common with the solemn and moving visions of Millet; the magic of Diaz, which transfigures a hunt into something wonderful and heroic, is beyond him; he is not so good a painter as Troyon, nor has he so large and true a sense of landscape. But he has represented the forms, the manners, the characters, the movements of certain animals in an environment of light and air and with effects of mystery and touches of poetry that make his work unique in painting.

---

69. Landscape with Sheep.

    A shepherdess keeping sheep in the shadow of a group of oaks. $8\frac{1}{2}$ by $13\frac{1}{4}$ inches. 21·50 by 35 centimètres. [1082.

Lent by JOHN WORDIE, Esq., Glasgow.

70. Le Retour du Troupeau.

    A shepherd, in a belted blouse, leaning on the half-door of a sheep-house, into which his flock is crowding before him. A black dog to the left. An effect of sunshine through the leafage of a small tree upon the group and the sheep-house wall. $20\frac{1}{2}$ by 25 inches. 52 by 63·50 *centimètres*. [1157.

ETCHING.   *Lent by* ALEXANDER BOWMAN, Esq., Edinburgh.

ALPHONSE LEGROS

BORN AT DIJON, 1837

T eleven years old Legros was apprenticed to a drunken house-painter in his native city. He attended the local school of art for some few months, and soon afterwards, migrating with his family to Lyons, found work at a decorator's, and was employed in the renovation of Cardinal de Bonald's chapel. His next stage was Paris, where he worked with Cambon, the scene-painter, a pupil of Ciceri; at the École des Beaux-Arts; with Belloc (1786-1866), a pupil of Regnault and Gros, in the Rue de l'École de Médecine; and, finally, with Lecoq de Boisbaudran (b. 1802) at the École Municipale de Dessin. In 1857 he exhibited a portrait of his father, and, albeit a kinsman, not of Courbet but of Holbein, was acclaimed by Baudelaire and Champfleury as a modern and a "realist." This work he followed up with an *Angélus* in 1859, an *Ex-Voto* in 1861, and a *Messe des Morts* in 1863; and about the time of the last, his success being anything but great, he came to England, where he has ever since remained. He was medalled at the Salon in 1866, for a *Lapidation de Saint-Étienne*, and, again, in 1868, the year at the Royal Academy of his *Demoiselles du Mois de Marie*, for an *Amende Honorable*. Other pictures of importance are the *Pèlerinage*, the *Bénédiction de la Mer*, the *Chaudronnier*, the *Repas des Pauvres*, the *Marchand de Poissons*, the *Jacob's Dream*; while among his innumerable etchings—it is claimed for him that after Méryon he has a principal share in the revival of the art—may be mentioned the *Procession dans les Caveaux de Saint-Médard*, the *Pêcheur à la Truble*, the *Mort du Vagabond*, the *Grands Arbres*, the *Coup de Vent*, the final version of *La Mort et le Bûcheron*, the *Canal*, the *Rivière*, the *Watts*, the *Dalou*, the *Manning*, the *Rodin*, the *Carlyle* called "l'Homme au Chapeau." Since 1876 he has been Slade Professor at University College, London; and of late,

exhibiting but rarely, he has contented himself with teaching his classes, and working for himself, not only in the several media proper to his art—oils, water-colours, etching, sepia, pencil, chalk—but as a sculptor and a medallist as well.

As I have said, he began as a so-called realist: but he has been described as "an Old Master belated," and from the first the description was appropriate. It is only in sentiment and choice of subject that he is a modern. The developments of Constable and his successors can scarce be said to exist for him. In his treatment of the figure he is inspired by the example of Holbein and Jehan Fouquet; in his landscapes he is a pupil of Nicolas Poussin; he touches hands with Van Dyck and Rembrandt in his etchings, and with Vittore Pisano in his medals. His colour, again—severe, solemn, chastened—is modern in no sense of the word; and the contrast between himself and his contemporaries is made more trenchant by the austerity of his ideals, his disdain of trick, the sustained dignity, the sobriety and the distinction, of his art. It has been said of him, and with truth, that he lacks charm, and seeks and finds too exclusively the beauty of ugliness. But it is also true that he is a consummate artist, whose influence for good can hardly fail to be enduring and profound.

71. Les Demoiselles du Mois de Marie.

The interior of a village church. To the left a monk at the organ, with a second in the act of conducting a choral service. To the right a congregation of peasant girls, seated for confirmation. 41 by 56½ inches. 1 mètre 40 centimètres by 1 mètre 43·50 centimètres. [1161.

Lent by CONSTANTINE A. IONIDES, Esq., London.

ANTONIO MANCINI

Born at Narni, 184—

THERE are no dates in Mancini's life, and with the surmise that he must have been born in one or other of the Forties, its chronological interest is exhausted. But there are not wanting details of another kind, and these, it must be owned, are picturesque enough. He is the son of a tailor, and while yet a boy he removed with his father from Narni—the scene of Corot's first exhibited landscape—to the neighbouring city of Naples. Here he worked for some time under Lista—who took him at last into his own studio, and made him a painter of fruit and flower pieces—and at the Fine Art Institute, where he had Piccini and Michetti for his fellow-students, and produced so many portraits and portrait-studies that he got to be called the Painter of Heads. His first essay in this branch of art was bought by Signor Morelli (Ivan Lermolieff), and later on he is said to have made a great hit with a portrait of his father. But buyers were scarce, and for some time his poverty was so black that, like Géricault before him, he was often glad to barter a picture for a clean canvas.

At last he had a stroke of luck. He attracted the notice of M. Albert Coën, and Fortuny remarked his work in the shop-windows, and began to buy of him. Then, on M. Coën's advice, he went to Paris, and stayed there for seven months, working for the Goupils, and making himself the fame among painters of one whose technical accomplishment is of the best. Of a second journey to the French capital, in company with his old friend, the sculptor Gemito, the issues were less prosperous. He got into difficulties with his employers; and when Gemito brought him back to Naples, his state of mind was such that his friends were compelled to place him under restraint. In the asylum he painted the portraits of his fellow-patients; and in course of time he recovered health, and went into the world once more.

At Rome, the scene of his next sojourn, he was well received by his fellows, who bought his pictures, and made much of him. It was not long before he fell seriously ill; but his energy is uncommon, and as soon as ever he was healed he returned to the pursuit of his art. At the time of writing he has made his head-quarters at Venice, where he has exhibited one of his finest portraits, and where he is even now engaged upon a larger and a more complex work—it is a picture of naked women—than any he has heretofore essayed.

Mancini is a painter's painter. We have seen that his first good work was bought by the most fastidious and acute of living critics, that Fortuny was one of his earliest patrons, and that many of his pictures have been purchased by men of his own calling—Mesdag, Villegas, Gérôme among others. The reason is not far to seek: Mancini is a master-craftsman. In his work the proportions of the literary and the plastic elements are as ·5 and 99·5 in the hundred. It is as a painter that he sees his subjects, and it is as a painter that he represents them. His care is only for appearances; and to record his observations he has invented as it were a shorthand of singular energy and expressiveness. His colour is very personal and daring; his brushwork has a peculiar significance; his management of paint is clearly the outcome of a special faculty. To the outsider, it may be, his work is neither suggestive nor agreeable; but to the expert it appeals as art triumphant over the technical difficulties which have been its principal inspiration.

72. **The Sick Child.**

A little girl in bed, wrapped in a black shawl, and holding a spray of yellow flowers. A pillow of greenish white, against a background of dark crimson, with a purple curtain to the left. 30 by 24½ *inches.* 76 by 62·33 *centimètres.* [1134.

Lent by H. W. MESDAG, Esq., The Hague.

LOUIS METTLING

Born at Dijon, 1847

METTLING comes of English parentage; but he was born a fellow-citizen of Legros and François Rude, and he is French by training, and French in accomplishment and ideal. He studied at Lyons at the École des Beaux-Arts, was a pupil of Cabanel, and has exhibited at the Salon; but in the Royal Academy no work of his has ever, I believe, been shown.

He is a painter pure and simple. For beauty, human interest, human sentiment, he cares little or nothing. But he is keenly alive to the suggestiveness of light and atmosphere, the pictorial quality of facts, the capabilities of paint, and, in a word, to whatever can display the especial powers of the medium in which he works. These are his tastes, and for these he is well equipt. His eye is quick, his hand uncommonly skilful, his judgment sound, his method masterly, his style of a sober brilliance. A modern as Velasquez is modern, he may be said to derive from that great master, and to be not unworthy his descent.

73. **Head of a Child.**

    A bust portrait of a child in a blue pinafore, against a background of plain red. 17½ by 14½ inches. 44·50 by 37 centimètres. [1094.

    Lent by ONE OF THE COMMITTEE.

74. **Still-Life.**

    A study of *bric-à-brac* grouped about a white china jar. Painted in a rich key of brown. 12¼ by 9¼ inches. 31 by 23·50 centimètres. [1115.

    Lent by ONE OF THE COMMITTEE.

METTLING 51

75. The Song.

An interior, with a man in mediæval costume singing to a mandolin. 17½ by 14½ inches. 44·50 by 37 centimètres. [1152.

Lent by ONE OF THE COMMITTEE.

76. Head of a Girl.

A bust portrait: the head in glowing relief against a background of rich brown. 21 by 17½ inches. 53·50 by 44·50 centimètres. [1129.

Lent by ONE OF THE COMMITTEE.

JEAN-FRANÇOIS MILLET

1814—1875

HE son of many generations of peasants, Millet was born at Gruchy, a little hamlet on the shores of La Hogue. Reared upon Virgil and the Bible, he learned to draw and paint for himself while working on his father's farm; and in 1837, after a certain schooling at Cherbourg, he was sent to Paris, at the expense of the former city. He drew for a time with Delaroche and in the Atelier Suisse. But his real teachers were the Old Masters in the Louvre, and especially Correggio, Nicolas Poussin, and Michelangelo—" celui qui me hanta si fortement toute ma vie." From the first he learned the processes of colour and modelling; from the second the principles of composition and the greater and severer attributes of style; and from the third the mystery of gesture and expression. Other influences were Rubens and Delacroix in one direction, and in another Mantegna, Angelico, and Filippo Lippi; and later on came Rembrandt and the great landscape painters contemporary with himself.

Painted to sell, his earlier pictures are frankly and naïvely sensuous. Their colour is rich enough to remind us that for years the painter was the friend and fellow-worker of Diaz; in modelling and chiaroscuro they are often admirable; they express, in terms that are often sumptuous and always beautiful, a liberal and healthy sentiment of the nude. It was not until Millet left Paris for Barbizon (1849) that he returned to the ideals of his youth, and became, by swift and easy stages, the epic painter of rusticity. At Barbizon, where he knew Rousseau, and where he laboured till his death, he began by producing his prodigious *Semeur*, which was exhibited in 1850, the year of Courbet's *Enterrement d'Ornans*. It was the first of a long line of masterpieces—the *Glaneuses*, the *Bûcheron et la Mort*, the *Homme à la Houe*, the *Meules*, the *Berger au Parc*, the *Vigneron au Repos*, to name but these—in which the new capacities of landscape, the conquests of Rousseau and Diaz and Constable, are found in combination with an heroic treatment of the figure. This development was Millet's work, and remains perhaps his chief contribution to pure art.

Both these elements are fused in so close an intimacy as to form but one interest, so that, pictorially considered, each work is a complete organic whole. But this is not all. Of most of them the effect is ethical as well as plastic. They are not simply works of art: they are as it were lay sermons in paint, for they embody ideas which, not absolutely literary in themselves, are to some extent susceptible of a literary expression. Millet, in fact, was not less poet than painter. The French peasant was his hero, the romance of man in nature his material. To his fellow-craftsmen, his work must always present extraordinary interest; for, while his gift was immense and his accomplishment in its way unrivalled, there have been few whose study of reality has been more searching and profound, and few the record of whose observations is so charged with brainstuff and so pregnant with significance. But he did not work for his fellow-craftsmen alone. He has touched the scenes of that "epic in the flat" which was his legacy to time with a dignity, a solemn passion, a quality of fatefulness, a sense of eternal issues, which lift him to the neighbourhood of Michelangelo and Beethoven, and make his achievement, like theirs, the possession of all mankind.

---

77. The Shepherdess.

A hollow, with trees and a glimpse of plain beyond. To the right, against the bank, a shepherdess. To the left, and in the centre, sheep. 7¾ by 12¼ *inches*. 20 by 31·50 *centimètres*. [1124.

Lent by CONSTANTINE A. IONIDES, Esq., London.

78. Going to Work.

Early morning in the plain of Barbizon. A young man and young woman going a-field: he with a fork on his shoulder, she with a basket on her head. A version of the etching. 21 *by* 17 *inches.* 53·33 *by* 43 *centimètres.* [1138.

Lent by JAMES DONALD, Esq., Glasgow.

79. L'Amour Vainqueur.

A band of *amorini* haling a girl, half-draped in blue, into the recesses of a wood. A warm background of trees and leafage. 18 *by* 15 *inches.* 45·50 *by* 38 *centimètres.* [1144.

Lent by JAMES STAAT-FORBES, Esq., London.

80. The Sheepfold.

A version in pastel—almost monochromatic—of the picture known as *Le Berger au Parc*. A fold, by moonrise, in the plain of Barbizon, into which the shepherd is passing his flock. 27¾ by 37 *inches.* 70·50 by 94 *centimètres.*
[1107.

Lent by JAMES DONALD, Esq., Glasgow.

81. **The Fisherman's Wife.**

Under a dark sky, streaked with yellow, a woman in a red skirt, a blue-grey jacket, and white headgear, seated among grey rocks, and gazing, head on hand, out to the left. 17½ by 14¼ inches. 44·50 by 36·33 centimètres. [1145.

Lent by H. W. MESDAG, Esq., The Hague.

82. Knitting.

Drawn in black chalk. A cottage interior; a woman guiding the hand and needles of a child knitting. 14 *by* 11½ *inches.* 35·50 *by* 29 *centimètres.* [1171.

Lent by JAMES STAAT-FORBES, Esq., London.

83. The Wood-Sawyers.

A glade in Fontainebleau forest. In the background, dimly seen, a woodman at work. In the foreground, a great tree-trunk which two men are sawing into circles. The general scheme is one of brown and green, in which the blue of the foremost sawyer's trousers explodes with a certain violence. 21¾ by 31 inches. 55·50 by 79 centimètres. [1131.

Lent by CONSTANTINE A. IONIDES, Esq., London.

ADOLPHE MONTICELLI

1824—1886

ORN in Marseilles, Monticelli was a pupil of Raymond Aubert (1781-1857), who made him a devotee of line, a fanatic of Raphael and Ingres. His conversion began (it is said) before a Delacroix, and was completed by the influence and example of Diaz, in whose neighbourhood, in Paris, he lived for some years, and whose manner he mimicked with such spirit and intelligence that his work was often sold for his master's. Returning south, he painted steadily, sold as fast as he produced, and amused himself with all his strength. It is the nature of the Provençal, as M. Daudet has shown, to admire what is eccentric and showy; and Monticelli—handsome, vigorous, eloquent, persuasive, uncommon—was of all painters the one for Provence. His fame grew legendary: he was not the lawful son of a gauger, but a bastard of the Gonzagas; the great Diaz had secluded him for many years to steal the secret of his colour; in truth there was not his like in the length and breadth of the Rhone Valley. His story has been but vaguely told; but it seems that to this period of triumph there succeeded one of desperate reverses for which nobody was responsible but Monticelli himself. A second sojourn in Paris, during which the painter was reduced to the necessity of selling his pictures from the pavement, and herding at night with vagabonds in waste lands and empty houses, ended in flight before the advance of Von Moltke. Monticelli had not only to tramp it to Marseilles, but for six-and-thirty days to paint his way from place to place. Settling in his native city, he adopted his final manner, and stood revealed as the painter of pure sensations, the colourist for colour's sake, who has perplexed and scandal-

ised so many critics. He gave the rein to his extraordinary faculty of improvisation, producing a picture a day, and selling his work for whatever it would bring. And year by year the paint grew thicker and less significant, the harmonic instinct more eccentric and uncertain, the intellectual quality more childish and obscure. It was said that, like Musset, he took to the worst drink of all—that his rare and admirable temperament was wrecked in absinth; it seems certain that in him, as in so many of the imperfectly gifted, the sensualist got and kept the upper hand of the artist. For some time before the end they were but few who knew if he were alive; his "painted music," his clangours of bronze and gold and scarlet, his triumphs of unrepresentative effect, had profited him so little.

With Monticelli the be-all and end-all of painting was colour. A craftsman of singular accomplishment, to tint and tone he yet subordinated drawing, character, observation—three-fourths of art. Delacroix and Turner used, it is said, to amuse themselves with arrangements in silks and sugar-plums; and what they did in jest, or by way of experiment, was done by the Marseillais in sober earnest, and as the last word of art. True it is that he has a magic —there is no other word for it—of his own: that there are moments when his work is infallibly decorative as a Persian crock or a Japanese brocade; that there are others when there is audible in these volleys of paint, these orchestral explosions of colour, a strain of human poetry, a note of mystery and romance, some hint of an appeal to the mind. As a rule, however, his art is purely sensuous. His fairy meadows and enchanted gardens are so to speak "that sweet word Mesopotamia" in two dimensions; their parallel in literature is the verse that one reads for the sound's sake only —in which there is rhythm, colour, music, everything but meaning. If this be painting, then is Monticelli's the greatest of the century. If it be not—if painting be something more than dabbling exquisitely with material—then, it has to be admitted, these fantasies materialised, these glimpses of the romance of colour, are only the beginnings of pictures—the caprices of a man of genius gone wrong. It is perhaps ungenerous to quarrel with an artist for giving no more than he chooses. But it is claimed for Monticelli that he is the greatest colourist of the century; and it is impossible to refrain from contrasting him with his predecessors on the throne, and from measuring the difference between his royalty and theirs.

Upon the present generation—which delights to confuse one art with another, which must have descriptive music, and will only take an interest in pictures that are disguised literature—the influence for good of Monticelli, of painting reduced to its simplest elements, is not a thing to be despised. The danger is that, once accepted, it may woo to excess in the opposite direction, and mislead the neophyte to ignore the primary essentials and despise the greater qualities of art. Man's capacity of enjoyment is limited; his capacity of idiosyncrasy—his hobby-horsical capacity—is not; and it is odds but if he feels in all its fulness the vague magic of Monticelli, he may think himself superior to the more varied and more complex enchantment of Raphael and Rubens. In art as in life, the undue development of a special faculty is fatal to the general growth. And what is true of those who make is true tenfold of those who only admire and feel. Where the artist only breaks his shins the amateur is pretty certain to break his neck.

84. Ladies in Garden.

A bevy of ladies, attended by a keeper with dogs. A background of deep blue-green and russet foliage. 10 by 12¾ inches. 25·50 by 32·50 centimètres.

[1150.

Lent by ARTHUR SANDERSON, Esq., Edinburgh.

85. The Fête.

In the foreground two horsemen and a bevy of ladies. To the right a bank with trees. In the background, under a blue sky, sandy mounds in strong sunshine. 15½ by 27½ inches. 39·50 by 70 centimètres. [1156.

Lent by DANIEL COTTIER, Esq., London.

86. Landscape : Gipsies.

A pass in the rocks, with towering crags to the right. In the foreground, on (apparently) a low wall, a seated female figure. 15 by 9½ inches. 38 by 24 centimètres.

[1170.

Lent by DANIEL COTTIER, Esq., London.

87. The Ravine.

With other figures mysteriously busy, a horseman turning in his saddle to look at two ladies reclining in the front of the picture. A "symphony in white and grey."   13¾ by 9½ inches.   35 by 24 centimètres.   [1116.

ETCHING.   Lent by DANIEL COTTIER, Esq., London.

88. Ladies in Garden.

Three groups of ladies, clad apparently in rainbows, and relieved against a background of chocolate brown. On the right a great silver vase. 13 by 17 inches. 33 by 43 centimètres.   [1080.

Lent by ONE OF THE COMMITTEE.

89. Ladies in Garden.

A suggestion of five ladies in gorgeous dresses in a torchlit garden. 13¼ by 17¾ *inches.* 33·50 *by* 45 *centimètres.* [1076.

Lent by THOMAS GLEN ARTHUR, Esq., Glasgow.

90. Landscape : Autumn.

A group of loves and ladies in a sunlit meadow, with a hem of winding river and a background of autumnal woods. In the centre a brown and golden tree. 15 *by* 23 *inches.* 38 *by* 58·50 *centimètres.* [1071.

Lent by ONE OF THE COMMITTEE.

91. **Landscape with Ladies.**

At the foot of a great tree, against a deep-blue distance, a group of ladies seated in a half-circle. To the right a bank with trees. 14¼ by 25½ *inches*. 36 by 64·50 *centimètres*.
[1084.

Lent by ARTHUR SANDERSON, Esq., Edinburgh.

PIERRE-ÉTIENNE-THÉODORE ROUSSEAU

1812—1867

NATIVE of Salins in the Jura was Claude Rousseau, a merchant tailor of good connection and unblemished repute; but his wife, Louise Colombet, was a Parisian, and it was in Paris, in what is now the Rue Aboukir, that Théodore, their only son, was born to them. Mme. Rousseau came of an artist family: her father was a working sculptor; her uncle, Gabriel Colombet, a pupil of David, achieved a certain success in portraiture; her cousin, the landscape painter, Alexandre Pau de Saint-Martin, first of the name, was a pupil of Carle Vernet (1758-1836), and exhibited pretty constantly at the Salon between 1791 and 1848. It was in the studio of this last that Théodore —who seems to have begun to draw as soon as he could hold a pencil, and whose sketches were an article of commerce among his school-fellows—first essayed himself in colour. He used, we are told, to copy the pictures on his uncle's walls; but, according to Sensier, he saw and painted them not as models to be reproduced, but as still-life objects in an environment of space and air. Sensier, indeed, would have us believe that his hero was interested in the phenomena of light at a period when these were, as he puts it, "complétement délaissées." But as Constable appeared upon the scene when Rousseau was but twelve years old, and as Delacroix and Bonington and Paul Huet were even then exploring in the same direction as their great forerunner, the claim may be dismissed as one of those which fall naturally enough from the biographer, but need give the historian no pause.

Before he was fifteen Rousseau had spent a great deal of time in the forest lands of Franche-Comté, in the heart of which the sculptor Maire, a friend of his father's, had set up a chain of sawpits. The enterprise failed; and when the boy returned to Paris, Claude Rousseau, whose connection was largely royalist and aristocratic, and who had been lucky enough during the Hundred Days to render a capital service to no less a man than Talleyrand, resolved to make him an engineer, and by Talleyrand's influence to enter him at the École Polytechnique. But Théodore had thought the matter over for himself, and was bent upon a career of his own election. Taking counsel of none, he bought himself colours and brushes, went out to Montmartre and made a sketch from nature, brought home his work, and took advantage of his parents' admiration and delight to ask permission to be a painter. The thing was submitted to Pau de Saint-Martin, who took the boy out sketching, applauded his ambition, and advised that he should be sent to learn his craft in the studio of Rémond (1795-1875). The experiment was foredoomed to failure. The master, a neo-classic of the stiffest type, practised landscape on the debased and half-obliterated lines of Poussin; the pupil, though he had seen nothing of Constable, whose acquaintance he is said to have made as late as 1832, had already entered upon his life-long struggle with nature; and between him and Rémond there was presently discord. "J'ai été plusieurs ans à me débarrasser des spectres de Rémond," said Rousseau later on; but it is evident that from the first he followed his own bent and studied in his own way. In fine weather he went into the country—to Sèvres, Meudon, Compiègne, Cernay, Saint-Cloud —and sketched in the open air; and when the weather was bad he copied Claude and Karel du Jardin in the Louvre, or drew from the living model under Guillon-Lethière (1760-1832), once the rival of David in painting, and in teaching of David's greatest pupil, Gros. To the bright and happy genius of Corot nothing ever came amiss; he adapted and assimilated with the royal facility of Raphael, or Molière, or Dumas; he could profit even by the tradition of Valenciennes and the lessons of Victor Bertin. Rousseau, his inferior in art, and in originality assuredly no more than his equal, was of a different temper. He was obstinately and suspiciously individual first and last; and when in 1830 he broke with his master, and went sketching for himself among the strange formations and the wild and troubled sites of Auvergne, he had learned not even the little Rémond could teach, and years afterwards was fain, as he confessed, to acquire the art of "engineering" (*machiner*) a picture from his friend and adviser, Jules Dupré.

The career on which he entered on his return to Paris from Cantal and the Puy-de-Dôme was destined to be curiously tortuous and irregular. In the beginning all went with him. Romanticism was in the gaudiness of full flower: it was the year of *Antony* and *Darlington* at the Porte-Saint-Martin and of *Marion Delorme* at the Théâtre-Français, of *Le Vingt-Huit Juillet* at the Salon and *Robert le Diable* at the Académie de Musique, of Balzac's *Peau de Chagrin* and Hugo's *Notre-Dame*, the *Atar-Gull* of Eugène Sue and the *Roi des Ribauds* of Paul Lacroix; and that Rousseau was a deserter from Rémond and a recreant from the faith of Rémond's gods was sufficient to secure attention to his aims, respect for his ideals, and unshrinking confidence in his capacity. His first Salons were those of 1831 and 1833; in 1834 he appears to have gained a medal, and sold his picture, a *Lisière de Bois*, to the Duke d'Orléans; in 1835 he was once more represented, and by a couple of *Esquisses*. Then the tide turned. To the Jury of 1836—Heim, Bidault, Ingres, Schnetz, the two Vernets, Paul Delaroche, Guérin, among others—he submitted his *Descente des Vaches*, a landscape with cattle painted from sketches made in the Jura; and, in company with Marilhat, Champmartin, Paul Huet, Louis Boulanger, Barye, and Delacroix, he was refused a place in the official exhibition. He remained without the gates till 1848; and but for the accident of a revolution and a change of government he might not have reconquered the right of way so soon.

His position during these twelve years of exile was distressing enough. Decamps, George Sand, Daumier, Delacroix were his admirers and wellwishers; Diaz, Ary Scheffer, Jules Dupré, the critic Thoré were the most diligent of his friends. Revered and commiserated on the one hand as one of the martyr-saints of Romanticism, he was execrated on the other as a sort of drunken helot. Sometimes he sold a picture, and more often than not he was free to paint and repaint his work at will. He was not of a happy disposition; and, as he took himself and his reverses with a certain solemnity, it is to be feared that he suffered much. Things were first mended for him by the advent of the Second Republic. The official jury was dismissed; the mob of painters took to self-government; and Rousseau was elected one of the jury of 1848, the first under the new dispensation. Then Ledru-Rollin, as head of the state, gave him a capital commission; and after a lifetime of anxious chastity, in the course of which—impelled thereto, as Sensier explains, "par une susceptibilité outrée de son caractère"—he declined the hand of a young lady to whom he was deeply attached, and who was very much in love with him, he threw in his lot with a *payse* of his who had cast herself on his protection, and retired for good and all to Barbizon. But there was an unworthy strain in him; and the passage from absolute failure to comparative success was not at first to his advantage. In 1849 he exhibited for the first time since his exclusion thirteen years before; he gained a First Class medal, but when he found that Jules Dupré, who had given him proof after proof of faultless friendship, had received the ribbon of the Legion of Honour, he professed himself affronted, refused to be appeased, and broke with his old comrade there and then. To the Salon of 1851 he sent six canvasses; but this year the ribbon fell to Diaz, and Rousseau, after charging the Hanging Committee with conspiracy, and being compelled to retract his accusation, gave out that he would exhibit no more. He kept his word until the Salon of 1852, where he was represented by an *Effet de Givre* and a *Paysage après la Pluie*, which gained him at last admission into the Legion. After this the circumstances of his life and the quality of his temper both improved. At the Exposition Universelle of 1855 he was splendidly conspicuous; he made money enough to pay Millet 4000 francs for his *Greffeur*; he had so far improved in temper and tact as to make the purchase not in his own behalf, but as the agent of a phantom rich American. In 1857 he had acquired sufficient importance to be made the victim of a sort of "knock-out" on the part of a Belgian dealer. In 1861 he sold a lot of twenty-five pictures and studies at the Hôtel Drouot for some 37,000 francs; in 1863 another lot of seventeen for close on 15,000 francs. Three years later Prince Demidoff commissioned him to paint two pictures for 10,000 francs apiece; while with MM. Brame and Durand-Ruel he did business to the extent of 140,000 francs, and after paying his debts was able to spend some 80,000 francs upon Japanese drawings and rare prints. In 1866 he was a member of the Salon Jury, and the Emperor's guest at Compiègne; and the year after he sent two pictures to the Salon, exhibited over a hundred sketches and studies at the Cercle des Arts, and was appointed President of the Jury at the Exposition Universelle, where he was represented by thirteen of his finest works. For these he was presently awarded one of the four Medals of Honour. The distinction, which he shared with MM. Cabanel, Meissonier, and Gérôme, was a tremendous blow to him. He had set his heart on officer's rank in the Legion; Corot, Pils, Gérôme, Jules Breton, and Français were gazetted without him; and the disappointment was more than he could endure. He was promoted after some little delay; but he had meanwhile been stricken with paralysis, and after a six months' agony he died in the December of the same year. Mme. Rousseau had long been hopelessly insane; we read of her capering and singing in the chamber of death, absolutely unconscious of bereavement.

Rousseau was not the poet of a site, the wooer of one only dryad. Insatiable of experience, greedy of discovery and conquest, he was for ever breaking new ground and opening up fresh provinces of material. As I have noted, he began by exploring the environs of Paris, and passed at a stride to the study of the peculiar features of Auvergne. He was at least twice in Normandy (1831 and 1832), where he studied the *Côtes de Granville* of his second Salon. In 1834 and 1861 he painted in the Jura, where he collected the material of his *Descente des Vaches* and his *Vue de la Chaîne des Alpes* (1867). In 1835-36 he went to Broglie, to paint a view of the castle, commissioned of him by the Duke as a gift for Guizot; and in 1837 he worked long in Brittany, the scene of the *Marais en Vendée* (called "la Soupe aux Herbes") and the *Avenue des Châtaigniers*. He was thrice with Jules Dupré in the Île-de-France (1841, 1845, and 1846), and among the booty which he brought back with him were the *Effet de Givre*, the *Lisière de Bois: Soleil Couchant*, and a famous *Avenue de Forêt*. From Berry (1842) he returned with the *Mare*, the *Curé*, the *Jetée d'un Étang après la Pluie*; from Gascony (1844), with the *Four Communal* and the *Marais dans la Lande*. But his favourite painting-ground was the Forest of Fontainebleau. He discovered it as early as 1833; year after year he lodged at Ganne's, the historic tavern, or in some peasant's cot, within easy distance of the Bas-Bréau and the Gorges d'Apremont; he set up his tent in Barbizon in 1848, and abode there until he died. Here Diaz was his pupil; here Jacque and Millet were his neighbours; here, as in a vast open-air studio, he matured his largest inspirations, resolved his knottiest problems, illustrated his boldest and richest effects. The forest has had no truer lover and no better painter. He saw it not as a crowd of trees, but as a monstrous organism, an enormous individuality; and he has rendered as none else has done the sense of its complex mystery and immensity, its infinite changefulness of colour and form, its multitudinous life, its impenetrable confusion of birth and death and increase and decay.

I have traced his wanderings in search of suggestion and experience with this particularity in order to show the range of his ambition, the originality of his experiments, the variety and novelty of his results. As a rule his method of production was painfully laborious and slow: the foundations of his pictures were constructed and made out with a reed pen in their smallest details; and on the formation thus provided stratum after stratum of paint was superimposed, until an end was gained, and he deemed that no more could be done. But the sum of his achievement is very large, and its quality is disconcertingly unequal. It may be that he caught at more than art could grasp; or it may be that his hand was only now and then the faithful servant of his brain; or it may be that he suffered from a sort of intellectual confusedness, and was fain to grope his way towards ideals that were dimly seen at first, and that shifted shapes as he advanced, as a mountain reveals itself under new aspects with every turn of the road. What is certain is that, while too often niggled and incoherent, "precious" yet inarticulate, at his best he is found to have not only originality of conception and sincerity and strength of sentiment, but a large and noble method, a singular power of expressing and evoking emotion, a magnificent gift of colour, an admirable majesty of style. Sensier tells us that, even in his darkest hours, it was hard for him to part with his works: he would keep them for years, and retouch and repaint till sometimes, as from the unknown masterpiece of Balzac's story, the "glory and the dream" had been painted quite away. It is natural, therefore, that his successors find him most consistently admirable in his *ébauches*—his "lay-ins"—and that the impression produced by the study of his life and aims and achievement is one of incompleteness. His art, indeed, has none of the consummate and triumphant mastery of Corot's. It is not seldom heroically inspired and irresistibly expressed; but it is mainly tentative and experimental, and it is often touched with failure.

92. Autumn Sunset.

A forest glade, with a group of oaks massed against a sunset sky. $8\frac{1}{4}$ by $11\frac{1}{2}$ inches. 21 by 29·33 *centimètres*. [1141.]

Lent by JAMES STAAT-FORBES, Esq., London.

FRENCH PICTURES

93. Landscape : Evening.

In the background a wooded hill, and in the foreground a road, with a village and trees, the whole scene bathed in the light of a fiery after-glow. 14¾ by 12½ inches. 37·50 by 32 centimètres. [1102.

Lent by THE HON. MR. JUSTICE DAY, London.

94. The Hunt.

A forest valley. In the centre a stream, with trees on the right bank. On the right a hunt of horsemen and dogs descending a slope. In the background a range of forest country, with an autumn evening closing over all. 8¼ by 11 inches. 21 by 28 centimètres. [1113.

ETCHING. *Lent by* ARTHUR SANDERSON, Esq., Edinburgh.

95. In the Forest of Clairbois, Fontainebleau.

On a hillock in the centre (middle distance), a tremendous mass of greenery, with a glimpse of the general forest beyond. On the right, in the near foreground, which is in deep shadow, a thin brown tree. A yellow light in the background and on one arm of the central group, with a sky of Titianic white and blue. 25¾ by 40¼ inches. 65·5 centimètres by 1 mètre 2 centimètres. [1146.

Lent by JAMES DONALD, Esq., Glasgow.

96. "Le Rageur."

Portrait study of a solitary oak. Autumn foliage against a background of heavy grey-black sky. The title is apparently a mistake, as, in these days at least, "Le Rageur" itself, a famous oak in the Gorges d'Apremont, bears (I am told) no resemblance whatever to the tree portrayed. 16 *by* 21 *inches*. 40·50 *by* 53·50 *centimètres*.
[1120.]

Lent by CONSTANTINE A. IONIDES, Esq., London.

97. A Storm.

In the foreground a flood; in the middle distance three dark trees, two partly submerged, with a ridge of upland running off to the left; in the background more drowned country, running up to, and lost in, a wild lightning-illumined sky. 9¼ *by* 12¼ *inches*. 23·33 *by* 31·20 *centimètres*. [1169.

Lent by CONSTANTINE A. IONIDES, Esq., London.

98. The Heath.

In the foreground, with a single figure, a sandy road leading into the picture through a level waste of grey scrub. A rainy sky of grey and blue, with a white light on a dark cloud to the right. 11¼ *by* 13 *inches*. 28·50 *by* 33 *centimètres*.
[1125.]

Lent by JAMES DONALD, Esq., Glasgow.

FERDINAND ROYBET

Born at Uzès, 1840

HIS artist began as an engraver, and studied his art under Vibert, Professor of Engraving at the Lyons École des Beaux-Arts (1799-1860). In 1866 he was medalled at the Salon, to which he has been a frequent contributor. Among his pictures, mention is made of a *Duo* and a *Fou sous Henri III.*; among his etchings, of a *Musicienne* and an *Intérieur de Cuisine*.

His principal merit is one of craftsmanship. He composes with intelligence, draws with spirit, and paints with a certain skill; his colour is taking, if a little garish; his inspiration is mainly literary and anecdotic, but his treatment is often pictorial. His art is popular with dealers and a certain type of amateur in the same way, and for somewhat similar reasons, as the art of Meissonier. Meissonier, indeed, like Hugo's Judge Jeffreys, "a fait des petits." One, and not the least, is Roybet.

99. The Winning Throw.

Two gamblers, in sixteenth century costume, playing dice on a board held on their knees. 19 *by* 23¼ *inches.* 48·33 *by* 59 *centimètres.* [1168.
Lent by MARIANO DE MURIETTA, Esq., London.

JOHN MACALLAN SWAN

BORN AT OLD BRENTFORD, 1847

BEGINNING at the Worcester School of Art, Mr. Swan was next a pupil of Mr. Sparkes at Lambeth, and a student in the Royal Academy. After a time he went to Paris (1874) and worked for four or five years with Gérôme; with Fremiet in the Jardin des Plantes; with Bastien-Lepage (1849-1885), Henecker, and Dagnan-Bouveret. Other influences were Matthew Maris in the present, and in the past Barye, Millet, and Delacroix. I shall have said enough if I add that Mr. Swan has not often exhibited, but that he was made a member of the Dutch Water-Colour Society in 1884, and awarded an Honourable Mention at the Salon of 1885.

It may be opined that he has not yet reached his full stature, or uttered his last word. Laborious, patient, slow to acquire and difficult to satisfy, his developments have been many. In his present stage he is less an individual growth than a result evolved by the operation of several influences. He knows whatever is to know; he has learned whatever can be taught; his training has been singularly liberal and exact; his accomplishment, in sculpture as in painting, is complete. But his inspiration is mainly voluntary and eclectic, his art a combination of perfections selected and assimilated from many different quarters. He constructs his animals with peculiar accuracy; the form, the character, the gesture are admirably realised; the environment, of light and air and scenery, in which they are placed is observed, and rendered, with a keen sense of the requirements of modern landscape and a full knowledge of the means by which they are to be met. The sentiment has never a touch of sham humanity or theatrical romance, but is always appropriate and sincere. And yet one feels that but for Millet, Barye, Delacroix, the art and the artist might well have been quite other than they are. It is only the formula that is new; the elements have served their turn in other hands. It is fair to add that the comparison provoked is never with third-rate men or inferior work. The artist is too learned and too strong, the art too solid and too sound. The difference is, *mutatis mutandis*, that between not Barye and Landseer, but Raphael and Nicolas Poussin.

100. **Lion and Lioness Prowling.**

Painted in water-colours. A desert landscape in the twilight, with a lion and lioness prowling side by side. 41 by 27½ *inches.* 1·2 *mètre by* 70 *centimètres.*

[1159.

Lent by ONE OF THE COMMITTEE.

CONSTANT TROYON

1810—1863

TROYON was born at Sèvres, where his father lived and laboured in the service of what was then the Manufacture Impériale. His first masters were his godsire Riocreux, a predecessor of Champfleury at the Musée de Céramique, and the respectable Poupart (born 1788), a pupil of Bertin; and under their guidance he began to walk in the ways of David.

One day, however, as he was sketching at Saint-Cloud, he fell in with one of the lesser lights of Romanticism in the person of the landscape-painter, Camille Roqueplan (1802-1855), who looked at his work, invited him to compare it with the study himself was making, denounced as false the gods upon whose knees he was being reared, and ended by making him acquainted with certain friends of his own, whose names were Théodore Rousseau, Camille Flers (1802-1868), Narcisse Diaz, and Jules Dupré. Troyon was not slow to profit by their teaching—especially that of Dupré; and in no great while he was recognised as one of the stoutest champions of the school. His advance was neither erratic nor slow. First seen at the Salon of 1832, he was the recipient of Third and Second Class medals in 1835 and 1840, of First Class medals in 1846 and 1848; of the Legion of Honour in 1849; and of another First Class medal at the Exposition Universelle of 1855, when he exhibited the *Bœufs allant au Labeur* by which he is represented in the Louvre.

He began with not cattle and sheep, but landscape pure and simple, and it was in that field that he won his earlier successes. Like Rousseau, he attempted subjects of several sorts, and went far and often afield in search of inspiration. He was found painting not only at Sèvres and Saint-Cloud and in the Forest of Fontainebleau, but in Brittany and the Limousin and all over Normandy; and it was a sketching tour in Holland that revealed his vocation to ·him, and, by determining a change of manner and theme, first set him in the way of immortality. Hitherto (1833-1846) he had been known for the violence of his colour, the truculent energy of his brush-work, his excesses in the abuse of paint. In the study of the Dutch masters—particularly, it is said, of Paul Potter and Rembrandt—he acquired a knowledge of saner principles, developed a capacity of better work, and discovered his fitness for the conquest of a new province in art; and after 1848 he was himself, he was Troyon the *animalier*, the greatest painter of sheep and cattle of his century. He had succeeded to his true inheritance, and he continued to enjoy it till his death. To say that he was very popular, and sold whatever he would, is to say that he produced much loose, careless, and indifferent stuff—that, in a word, he was no more above pot-boiling than Corot, Velasquez, or Van Dyck. But he did great work as well; and his good things are numbered with the art treasures of the world.

His Romanticism was but an effect of example and the headiness of youth. Having sown his wild oats, and passed through his time of *Sturm und Drang*, he returned to the contemplation of nature with eyes renewed and novel understanding; and he recorded a set of impressions distinguished by rare sincerity of purpose and directness of insight in a style of singular breadth, vigour, and felicity. His drawing is loose and inexact; and he composes not as an inheritor of Claude, but as a contemporary of Rousseau. But he had the true pictorial sense; and if his lines are often insignificant and ill-balanced, his masses are perfectly proportioned, his values are admirably graded, his tonality is faultless, his effect is absolute in completeness. His method is the large, serene, and liberal expression of great craftsmanship; and with the interest and the grace of art his colour unites the charm of individuality, the richness and the potency of a natural force. His training in landscape was varied and severe; and when he came to his right work, he applied its results with almost inevitable assurance and tact. He does not sentimentalise his animals, or concern himself with the drama of their character and gesture. He takes them as components in a general scheme; and he paints them as he has seen them in nature—enveloped in atmosphere and light, in an environment of grass and streams and living leafage. His work is not to take the portraits of trees or animals or sites, but, as in echoes of Vergilian music, to suggest and typify the country: with its tranquil meadows, its luminous skies, its quiet waters, and that abundance of flocks and herds at once the symbol and the source of its prosperity.

101. Landscape with Cattle.

A road beside a lake, with sheep and cattle, the central group in relief against three dark trees. An effect of soft, warm, low-toned sunshine. 25 by 38 inches. 63·50 by 96·50 centimètres. [1092.

Lent by CHARLES WARING, Esq., London.

102. Fishing-Boat off Honfleur.

A cutter-rigged boat on a rough green sea, shown in relief against a flaring orange sunset, which breaks through piles of black clouds, and shines through the foot of the sail. From the zenith downwards a sky of deep green-blue, flaked with tawny clouds. 23½ by 14 inches. 59·50 by 35·50 centimètres. [1140.

Lent by THOMAS GLEN ARTHUR, Esq., Glasgow.

103. Landscape with Sheep.

Four sheep feeding in a meadow, bordered by a reedy ditch. 11¼ by 20½ *inches.*
28·50 *by* 52 *centimètres.* [1078.

Lent by JAMES DONALD, Esq., Glasgow.

VICTOR VINCELET

CONCERNING this painter I can only find that he was born, like Marilhat, at Thiers, in the Puy-de-Dôme; that he was a pupil of a certain Hullier, and — it is said — of Antoine Vollon; that he exhibited at the Salons of 1869 and 1870; that he committed suicide some time in 1871; and that a picture of his, a *Fruits et Fleurs*, was bought for the gallery at Saint-Étienne.

Had he lived, there can be little doubt that he would have been distinguished. His colour is good; his values are extremely just; his brushwork is remarkable for vigour and suggestiveness; he had an excellent sense of air, a good knowledge of the qualities of light, and he painted flowers with a gusto and a sentiment that seem to me quite individual.

104. Flowers.

An arrangement of powerful colour-touches, suggesting rather than realising a handful of flowers strewn hap-hazard upon a table. 14¾ by 17½ *inches.* 36·50 by 44·50 *centimètres.* [1097.

Lent by ONE OF THE COMMITTEE.

ANTOINE VOLLON

Born at Lyons, 1833

NTOINE VOLLON—"le Chardin de nos jours"—is in the main self-taught. He studied engraving at the École des Beaux-Arts in his native city; and there is no doubt that he might have been a master of the craft. But he took naturally to painting, and his earliest ventures—a *Pierrot*, a portrait-picture, and so forth—were successful enough to send him to Paris almost ere he was out of his teens.

He was born under a fortunate star, and his apprenticeship was of the briefest. His first attempt upon the Salon Jury—with a *Portrait d'Homme*—resulted in exclusion. But in 1864 he not only exhibited two pictures, an *Art et Gourmandise* and an *Intérieur de Cuisine*, but sold the latter to the city of Nantes; and thereafter he proceeded from triumph to triumph. In 1865 he was medalled; in 1866 his *Singe à l'Accordéon* was bought for the gallery at Lyons; he was medalled a second time in 1866, when his *Curiosités* was sent to the Luxembourg, and yet again in 1869; in 1870 he gained the red ribbon with the famous *Poissons de Mer*, by which he will one day be represented in the Louvre; in 1872 and 1874 he exhibited the *Chaudron* and the *Coin de la Halle*, and sold them both to his native town; 1875 was the year of the *Armures* and the *Cochon Écorché*, 1876 was that of the *Femme du Pollet*; and in 1878 he was awarded a First Class medal for his *Casque de Henri II.*, and was promoted to officer's rank in the Legion of Honour. Since then he has exhibited, among other things, the *Courges* of 1880, the *Poteries* and the *Vue de Tréport* of 1886, and the *Port de la Joliette* of the present year. All these are in oil; but he is the artist of innumerable water-

colours, ranking with the good things of their kind, and forming by no means
the least remarkable feature in a remarkable achievement.

Vollon is a master-craftsman. His colour is rich, spontaneous, and individual, his drawing at once suggestive and exact; while in his brushwork—
large, vigorous, expressive—there is the gusto of the born painter. It is
fair to add that his range is not nearly so narrow as at first sight may
appear. The *Femme du Pollet*, the *Pierre Piachat* (1868), the *Espagnol*
(1878), are essays in the presentment of human character and the human form;
the *Port de la Joliette* is a picture of moving ships and blue water, of sunshine
and sea air and marine architecture. But his best work has been done in still-
life. In man and in landscape there is always character, and there is always
form: they possess an interest apart from that of paint; it is enough to
show them as they are by means of accurate drawing and representative colour.
The case is far other with flowers and fruit, with copper stewpans and joints
of meat and the textures of fur and feather. Either they must be left alone,
or they must be pictorially seen and pictorially treated. To render the facts
of them grain by grain, or hair by hair, or petal by petal, is to play a losing
match with the camera. Imitation for its own sake is the basest of aims, and
the pursuit of it can have but the meanest of results. In Vollon's art, as in
Chardin's, the quality of literalism is the last of which the artist has
dreamed. He sees and renders his subjects as a painter pure and simple—
as parts of a whole whose other components are immaterial and intangible.
The question with him is not one of textures and surfaces, but of the
presentation of light, the suggestion of air, the differentiation of values, the
development of plane on plane and gradation after gradation in obedience
to the requirements of modelling, the pictorial record (in a word) of the
innumerable operations of the environing medium of whatever exists as
material for art. To put the matter in other terms, he stands in the same
relation to the successors of Constable as Chardin stood to those of Hobbema
and De Hooch. He treats his armours and his piles of fish, his bowls of
strawberries and dead birds and groups of pots, precisely as an open-air painter
deals with clouds and distances and trees. The sun shines on them, and the
wind blows; they are localised in space, and shown together with the facts
of their unseen yet all-important envelopment. His still-lifes, indeed, have
been described as "des paysages d'intérieur," and the phrase is neither

infelicitous nor untruthful. They have the essential qualities of good modern landscape; and to marvel that the painter of *la Joliette* and the *Vue de Tréport* should also be the painter of the *Poissons de Mer* and the *Cochon Écorché*, were to betray a complete want of insight into what is best in all four.

---

105. Strawberries.

A table, with a white bowl of strawberries and a yellow pear, set against a background of dark brown-grey. 12¼ by 15½ *inches.* 31 by 39·50 *centimètres.*

[1106.

Lent by THOMAS GLEN ARTHUR, Esq., Glasgow.

FÉLIX-FRANÇOIS-GEORGES-PHILIBERT ZIEM

BORN AT BEAUNE, 1821

HE most nomadic and adventurous of painters is Ziem. As soon as he could, he left the Côte d'Or for Paris, and studied there for some years. But for him, as for Marilhat and Fromentin and Decamps, France was a world too narrow; and at four-and-twenty he started for Italy and the East. He was absent for some three or four years; and on his return, he sent to the Salon of 1849, which was his first, a *Vue du Bosphore* and a *Grand Canal de Venise*. He was medalled (Third Class) next year for a *Vue de Meudon*, and in 1852, having meanwhile gone the round of Holland, he gained a First Class medal with his *Chaumière à la Haye*. In 1854 he was represented by a *Port de Marseille*; in 1855 his *Vue d'Anvers* was purchased by the State, and he was awarded another Third Class medal; in 1857 he was decorated for a *Constantinople*; he exhibited a *Damanhour* and a *Gallipoli* in 1859, a *Tripoli* and a *Tamaris* in 1863, a *Stamboul* in 1864, a picture from the Camargue in 1865, a *Vue de Marseille* in 1868. This was his last appearance anywhere. In 1878 he was promoted to the rank of officer in the Legion of Honour; but with the Salon of ten years before his public life had come definitely to an end.

In 1860, Sensier tell us, Ziem had as many as four studios. Three were in France—at Paris, at Barbizon, and at Martigues in the Crau. The fourth, however, was at Venice, of which city Ziem has been from the first as it were the painter-in-ordinary. He broke ground, as we have seen, with a picture of the Grand Canal; he exhibited a *Soir à Venise* in 1854, a *Fête à Venise* in 1855, a *Place de Saint-Marc* in 1857, a set of *Vues de Venise* in 1861, a *Venise* in 1865, a *Venise: Soirée de Septembre* in 1866, a *Bucentaure*, a *Venise le Soir*, and a *Venise le Matin* in 1867; to his last Salon he sent a *Venise: Partie de Plaisir;* he has drunk the inspiration of innumerable water-colours from the same fair, enchanted cup. It is only natural that he should here be represented by a Venetian moonlight.

He was a friend of Rousseau, with whom he painted for some time at Barbizon, and who described him as "a Zoroastrian"—as "un Parsis enchanté de la lumière orientale." We read in Sensier how he bought a famous old windmill—the "Moulin de la Galette"—from Montmartre, which is one of the cradles of modern landscape, with a view to preserving it as a relic, and of transporting it to Barbizon, and rebuilding it for use as a studio. The plan fell through, or there might be something to say of Rousseau's influence upon its author. As it is, the pair have little in common save their delight in travel and the exploration of new sites. For Ziem, though he proceeds from a great school, is by no means a great painter. His manner is facile, elegant, engaging; his colour agreeable and decorative; his observation is rather superficial than searching, his sentiment neither moving nor profound. But he has the gift of charm; and his rendering of his impressions of nature is seldom found wanting in some of the better qualities of art.

---

106. Moonlight: Venice.

Moonrise on a canal in Venice, between two rows of tall houses, one of them —that on the left—illumined by torchlight without and by lamplight within. 25½ by 13½ *inches.* 65 *by* 34·33 *centimètres.* [1148.

Lent by ANDREW J. KIRKPATRICK, Esq., Glasgow.

DUTCH PICTURES

DAVID-ADOLPHE-CONSTANT ARTZ

BORN AT THE HAGUE, 1837

RTZ was a student first of all at the Amsterdam Academy, and afterwards in Paris, where he worked for eight years (1866-1874) under various masters. In 1873 he gained a Bronze medal at Vienna; in 1879 he was made a Knight of the Oaken Crown; he received an Honourable Mention at the Salon of 1880, and a Gold medal at the International and Colonial Exhibition, Amsterdam, in 1883. He is represented in the Rÿksmuseum, and in the Museum Booymans, Rotterdam. Among the best of his many pictures are the *Orphanage at Katwÿk*, the *Chaude Journée*, and the *Moment Propice*, all three of which are popular in *photogravure*.

He considers himself a pupil of Israels, though he has never worked in that painter's studio or under his immediate direction. Like Israels, indeed, he is interested in human character and sentiment, and like Israels he has sought and found his material in the types and circumstances of his native environment. But he has never sounded such deeps of emotion as have been revealed to his master; his view of character and life is apt to be a little superficial; his practice of art is often merely agreeable. He is the author of much that seems to have been done to sell; but at his best he is a good craftsman, with a real gift of colour, some feeling for light and air, and that directness of touch which marks the painter.

---

107. The Music Lesson.

> A blue-green interior. On the right a lady in grey; on the left a man in black; and in the centre a child in yellow, seated at a piano in vandyke brown, with a white sheet of music in relief against it. 25¼ by 31½ inches. 64 by 80 centimètres. [1011.
>
> *Lent by* DANIEL COTTIER, Esq., London.

BERNARDUS JOHANNES BLOMMERS

BORN AT THE HAGUE, 1845

LOMMERS, who was educated at the Hague Academy under Koelman (1820-1857), has been the recipient of two Gold medals, one at his birthplace (1875) and one at Amsterdam (1877), and of a Diploma of Honour at the International and Colonial Exhibition in the latter city in 1883.

Like so many others of his generation, he is in some sort a follower of Israels, as, in a greater degree, and perhaps to better purpose, he is a pupil of the great Dutchmen of the seventeenth century. Though the personal note is often absent from his work, it is distinguished, alike in oils and water-colours and etching, by sane technical qualities, by genuine sincerity of vision and simplicity of sentiment, and by an intelligent appreciation of the sounder and more important characteristics of modern art.

---

108. **Girl and Child.**

Painted in water-colours. A young woman (half-length), with a baby on her arm, seated at a table, and stirring a pot which is simmering on a pan of charcoal placed thereon. The general tone is grey, with touches of green on the pot, brown on the woman's hair, and blue on her apron. 22 *by* 15 *inches.* 56 *by* 38 *centimètres.* [1007.

ETCHING. *Lent by* JOHN WORDIE, Esq., Glasgow.

JOHANNES BOSBOOM

BORN AT THE HAGUE, 1817

OF Bosboom little is told, save that he learned his art off Philippus Jacobus Van Brée (1786-1871), himself a pupil of his brother Mattheus (1773-1839) at Antwerp and of Girodet (1767-1824) in Paris; that he is a Knight of three Orders—the Leopold, the Oaken Crown, and the Lion of the Netherlands; that he was medalled at the Exposition Universelle, Paris, in 1855, and again at the Centennial Exhibition, Philadelphia, in 1876; and that among the more famous of his pictures are a *Breda Church: The Tomb of Engelbert II.*, and a *Protestant Church at Amsterdam*, both of which themes he has repeated more than once.

He is a painter of daylight—above all, of daylight as it were domesticated: of its appearance when it is lodged between the confines of four walls, its effects upon architectural features and the colours and the lines of furniture. His early work is only exact and literal: his subjects were mostly church interiors, which he rendered with laborious accuracy of detail and minuteness of finish. Then, having disciplined his hand and mastered his material, he became an artist: his touch grew free and bold, his drawing instinct with expression, his treatment energetic and personal, his colour refined, distinguished, and suggestive; and he began to convey in terms of exquisite sobriety his sense of the all-pervading influences of atmosphere and daylight. Working indifferently in water-colours and in oils, he attained to a singular mastery of both; and though it has not always pleased him to do well in either—though, to put the matter bluntly, he is responsible for a great number of bad pictures—it may be said of him with a certain show of truth that his best is unique in art. None, perhaps, has had so keen and just an apprehension of the plastic quality of an interior as Johannes Bosboom; and none perhaps has revealed so much of its pictorial significance, or struck from its suggestions a note of such peculiar yet engaging romance. Of course he is a development; for is not Holland the birthplace of painted light? But he is so little the slave of his greater predecessors, of Rembrandt as of Pieter de Hooch, that he eliminates all human interest from his work. It is quite without reference to their relation to man, it is wholly for themselves, that he paints his cottage corners and his vast and lofty aisles. To him they are all-sufficient: as the troubled skies and green meadows of his native Suffolk were to Constable, as to Corot the quiet waters and the dawning skies of Ville d'Avray. And to present them as he sees them through the exquisite gradations of their aërial envelope is for him the only function of art.

109. Interior.

A church interior, cold and gaunt, illuminated from a window on the right. 9¾ by 7⅜ inches. 24·75 by 18·33 centimètres. [995.

Lent by THE HON. MR. JUSTICE DAY, London.

110. Interior of a Church.

Painted in water-colours. A view from the side aisle looking obliquely across the nave. In the foreground, at the foot of a pillar, two figures, one of them in black, which complete the harmony of a scheme in warm grey and white, with notes of brown in the wood-work. 15¾ by 12 *inches.* 40 by 30·50 *centimètres.* [998.

Lent by ONE OF THE COMMITTEE.

111. The Byre.

Painted in sepia. Interior of a stable, with a straw-heap lit with one yellow gleam from a window on the right. 8½ by 13¼ *inches.* 21·50 by 33·50 *centimètres.*
[1002.

Lent by ONE OF THE COMMITTEE.

112. Interior of Church.

Sketch-interior of a cathedral: with a great loft of timber to the left, the floor crowded with figures, and at the end a lighted window. A scheme of amber and yellow. 21½ by 16 inches. 54·50 by 40·50 centimètres. [1014.

Lent by DANIEL COTTIER, Esq., London.

113. Village on Sandhills.

Painted in water-colours. A village street, in pale grey and red, with a flat landscape in the distance. 8½ by 13¼ inches. 21·50 by 33·50 centimètres. [1042.

Lent by JOHN S. URE, Esq., Helensburgh.

114. Interior.

A lofty rood-screen with the tower in dark relief against the nave, which is lit from the west window. In front the chancel, with stalls of rich brown, and to the left a bishop's throne with scarlet curtains. 16¾ by 13½ inches. 42·50 by 34·50 centimètres. [1041.

Lent by PERCY WESTMACOTT, Esq., Newcastle-on-Tyne.

115. Interior.

Painted in water-colours. A church: against a white pillar, at the foot of which are two figures, the pulpit and sounding-board. 10 by 7¾ inches. 25·50 by 19·75 centimètres. [1067.

Lent by JOHN WORDIE, Esq., Glasgow.

116. Interior of Church.

Painted in water-colours. A cathedral aisle, illuminated from a great window at the end with a misty, yellow half-light, against which, in full relief, is painted a massive loft of black wood. In the middle distance is a procession bearing torches, and there are other figures scattered about the floor. 19 *by* 15 *inches.* 48·50 *by* 38 *centimètres.* [1020.

ETCHING. *Lent by* ONE OF THE COMMITTEE.

117. Interior.

Painted in water-colours. A cathedral aisle: with a cardinal and other figures in the middle distance, touched with light from a tall window on the left. A scheme of warm grey, with a faint hint of red. 15¼ *by* 11½ *inches.* 38·50 *by* 29·25 *centimètres.*
[1003.
Lent by PERCY WESTMACOTT, Esq., Newcastle-on-Tyne.

118. Church Interior.

Painted in water-colours. A rood-screen relieved against the nave, which is lit from the west window. In the foreground woodwork and figures. 14¼ *by* 10¼ *inches.* 36·33 *by* 26 *centimètres.* [1064.
Lent by JOHN A. CAMPBELL, Esq., Glasgow.

119. **Interior with Figures.**

Painted in water-colours. An empty stable: with a woman and child feeding chickens. A scheme of sepia, monochromatic save for a touch of red on the sleeve of one of the figures, and one of yellowish green through a window on the right-centre. 14¼ by 22 *inches.* 36·33 by 56 *centimètres.* [1055.

Lent by Ex-LORD PROVOST URE, Glasgow.

120. **A Convent Kitchen.**

Painted in water-colours. The interior of a convent kitchen, with a great fireplace to the left, a table with a sitting monk hard by, and a long dresser running down the centre with a black-robed figure at work at it. 15¾ by 21½ *inches.* 40 by 54·50 *centimètres.* [1057.

Lent by ROBERT RAMSEY, Esq., Glasgow.

121. **A Dutch Street.**

Painted in water-colours. A street with figures. A scheme of light grey and pale red. 13¼ by 9½ *inches.* 33·50 by 24 *centimètres.* [1024.

Lent by ONE OF THE COMMITTEE.

PAUL-JEAN CLAYS

BORN AT BRUGES, 1819

CLAYS'S master, Théodore Gudin (1802-1880), the fellow-worker of Isabey and Delacroix, exhibited in 1822 at the Salon of the *Dante et Virgile*, was medalled two years afterward, and was *décoré* as early as 1828; so that Clays himself, for all his Belgian origin, and the strong tendency towards "old masterism" revealed by his work, may fairly be said to have been a practical Romanticist, and to have had a share in the actual conduct of the movement. Like his master he has always painted marine and river scenes; and like his master he has had his fill of decorations and rewards. Beginning in 1844, in 1867 he sold his *Temps de Grain* to the King of the Belgians, who gave him the Order of Leopold, and he gained a Second Class medal at the Exposition Universelle; in 1875, the year of his *Calme par un Temps Orageux* and *La Tamise aux Environs de Londres*, he received the red ribbon; he was awarded another Second Class medal at the Exposition Universelle of 1878, where he was represented by five pictures, the *Rade de Dordrecht* and the *Calme dans le Haring-Vliet* among them; and in 1881 he was promoted to officer's rank in the Legion of Honour.

He is an accurate and devout observer; and he records his impressions, which are by no means lacking in variety, always with ease, often with breadth and vigour, and sometimes with a touch of genuine poetry. His colour is a trifle cold; but his pictures are usually agreeable decoration. His art, which has little trace in it of Gudin, is doubtless a survival; but the tradition it represents—and not unworthily—is that of Adrian Van de Velde, and Adrian Van de Velde was in his way a great painter.

122. On the Scheldt.
 A river, with windmills and houses on the right bank, and in mid-stream two smacks under sail. 11 *by* 18 *inches*. 28 *by* 45·50 *centimètres*. [1015.
 Lent by JAMES STAAT FORBES, Esq., LONDON.

JOSEF ISRAELS

BORN AT GRONINGEN, 1824

SRAELS learned his art in Amsterdam, at the Academy under Pieneman (1809-1861) and in the studio of Kruseman (1804-1862), and in Paris in the *ateliers* of Picot (1786-1868) and Henri Scheffer (1798-1861), a younger brother of the painter of the *Femmes Souliotes* and the *Francesca da Rimini*. He was already well known in Belgium and Holland when he broke ground in Paris, at the Exposition Universelle of 1855, with a picture (which is believed to be his only essay in the department of history) representing an incident in the life of the first William of Orange. To the Salon of 1857, having meanwhile discovered his vocation, and begun to paint at Katwÿk, he sent his *Children of the Sea* and his *Evening on the Shore;* at that of 1861 he was represented by no less than five examples of his art, and at that of 1863 by a group of three. After this he crossed the channel, and was produced at Burlington House, where in 1875 he exhibited his *Waiting for the Herring-Boats* and his *Returning from the Fields*. In 1867 he gained a Third Class medal, together with the ribbon of the Legion of Honour, with his famous *Interior of the Orphan Asylum at Katwÿk*. For his officer's cross he had to wait some years but he got it at last, and a First Class medal to boot, in 1878, when he appeared in the Champ de Mars as the author of four canvasses — the *Anniversary* and the *Village Poor* among them. Other notable works of his are the *Sleepers* (1867), the *Fishermen Disembarking* (1869), the *Sewing School at Katwÿk* (1881), *Silent Company* (1882), *Fine Weather* and the *Struggle for Life* (1883), and *Quand on devient Vieux* (1886), in painting; and in etching the plates entitled *La Soupe*, the *Smoker*, the *Fisherman*, and the *Sleeping Child*. The list might be extended almost indefinitely, for Israels is a man of indefatigable industry, and the sum of his achievement, in water-colours as in oils, grows larger day by day.

He is essentially a painter of man and man's emotions. Whatever their intrinsic merit, his landscapes and interiors are only settings for the human figure; however justly observed and brilliantly rendered, his effects of light are always subordinate to, and illustrative of, an interest of character and sentiment. He is a good painter of popular subjects; and it is not nearly so much because he is a good painter as because his subjects are popular that his renown is world-wide, and there is scarce a gallery of modern pictures but contains an example of his art. It is infinitely to his honour—it attests the incorruptible quality of his artistic sincerity—that, with all the applause that has been his, he should have remained his own severest critic, and have gone on improving as he has gone on painting. First and last, however, his real master has been not Kruseman or Picot, but the magician of the *Night Watch* and the *Syndics*; and to be maintained at such a height of emulation is to find rest impossible. This has been the happy fortune of Israels. His early work—a trifle violent in colour, somewhat strained in composition, in illumination arbitrary, in execution laboured and painful—is only so much unskilled and second-hand Rembrandt. But, as I have said, he has been always hard to please; and it is the practice of years that has made him the admirable craftsman of his greater pictures. Here his colour is individual, spontaneous, even rich, and his brushwork large and vigorous; his drawing, if a little loose and vague—as of a Millet indifferent to Poussin and unconscious of the antique—has a fine quality of suggestiveness; his light is clear, fluent, impalpable, remote from paint; his shadows are floating and luminous; often mannered and often naïvely naturalistic, his compositions are simply and effectively pictorial. It is small wonder if in Holland he has been a leader in the revival of art, and if his influence is felt in some degree throughout the painting of the world.

He is a master of pathos. The emotion is one easily strained; and always to produce it aright and of the purest quality is in these days impossible. It is apt to degenerate into mawkishness and twaddle; it is subject to the taint of affectation; when its flow is readiest and fullest, there oftentimes is its expression least to be encouraged—for to "pipe the eye" is only now and then a creditable proceeding, and to pipe the eye on any and every provocation is to put oneself outside the pale of art, and stand forth the fit exponent of no more in nature than is feeble and contemptible. Even with Shakespeare the

thing is sometimes theatrical; even with Dickens it is often whining in tone and unveracious in fact; one is not always too sure of it in Millet himself—for example, one cannot always wholly acquit him of a community of aim with Édouard Frère. Israels is neither Millet nor Dickens—still less is he Shakespeare; and it has to be admitted that his exercises in the pathetic are very often merely repellent. As a rule his appeal is all-too obvious. He makes no secret of his design upon your tears. On the contrary, he asks you to sit down and have a good cry with him; and he tells you plainly, not only that it will do you good, but that you will really enjoy it—that you will find it a luxury and a lesson in one. Sometimes it is impossible not to decline his invitation—not to resent it with scoffs and sneers. But on occasion his pathos is touched, both in conception and in execution, with a certain homespun dignity; and then he is fairly irresistible. He is not a great poet like Millet; neither in idea nor in utterance has he ever a touch of the heroic. But he has realised that it is man's destiny to suffer and endure, and he conveys this moral in terms that go straight to his hearers' hearts.

123. The Cottage Madonna.

A cottage interior lighted from a window to the right: with a comely young woman feeding her baby with pap. 51½ by 38¼ inches. 1 mètre 30·50 centimètres by 97 centimètres.
[999.

Lent by ALEXANDER YOUNG, Esq., London.

124. The Sleeping Child.

' A cottage interior lighted from a window in the centre. At a table an elderly woman, apparently a fisherman's wife, with a baby in her lap. A delicately graded scheme of greenish grey, the effect of which is heightened by the warmer tone of the table, the floor, and the roof, and by the introduction of three touches of red—in certain pots by the fireside, in a dish on the table, and in a handkerchief to the left. 48 by 61 inches. 1 mètre 22 centimètres by 1 mètre 55 centimètres.
[1030.

ETCHING.   *Lent* by THOMAS GLEN ARTHUR, Esq., Glasgow.

125. The Evening of Life.

A cottage interior, with an old woman seated in an arm-chair and looking out of the window. A scheme of rich dark brown, with a background of mellow brown and green, and a touch of red on the brick floor. 6¾ by 9½ inches. 17·33 by 24 centimètres. [1063.

Lent by JAMES STAAT-FORBES, Esq., London.

126. For These and All Thy Mercies.

A cottage interior lighted from a window at the back, beneath which, at a plain deal table, are seated an old woman and a young man, with a dish of potatoes between them. The title appears to be a misnomer, as both mother and son are crushed with grief. 40 by 66½ inches. 1 mètre 1·50 centimètres by 1 mètre 69 centimètres. [1019.

Lent by JAMES STAAT-FORBES, Esq., London.

127. The Pancake.

A cottage interior, with the housewife pouring batter into a frying-pan, and her two children sitting on the floor and watching the proceeding. 18 *by* 26 *inches.* 46 *by* 66 *centimètres.* [1053.

Lent by ANDREW MAXWELL, Esq., Glasgow.

128. The Grandfather.

Painted in water-colours. A cottage interior lighted from a window on the right, at which is seated an old man with a child upon his knees. 26 *by* 18 *inches.* 66 *by* 45·50 *centimètres.* [1039.

Lent by THOMAS GLEN ARTHUR, Esq., Glasgow.

DUTCH PICTURES

129. Woodland, with Figure.

Painted in water-colours. A lady reading, on a bench under trees. A scheme of greenish grey and blue. 7¾ by 8¾ inches. 20 by 22·33 centimètres. [1066.

Lent by ANDREW MAXWELL, Esq., Glasgow.

130. Landscape : Sheep in Moonlight.

A boy driving five sheep for the night into a stable, through a door held open for them by a little girl. 15½ by 27¾ inches. 39·50 by 70·50 centimètres. [1021.

Lent by JAMES STAAT-FORBES, Esq., London.

JOHANNES BARTHOLDUS JONGKIND

BORN AT LATDORP (OVERYSSEL), 1819

THE master of Jongkind, Eugène Isabey, the marine and landscape painter (1804-1886), is one of the most original and distinguished painters of the great Romantic group. He gained First Class medals in 1824 (his first Salon) and 1827; he received the ribbon of the Legion in 1852, and the officer's cross in 1852; he attained to First Class honours again in 1855; he was well and largely represented at the Exposition Universelle of 1878. His work—in colour, handling, inspiration essentially *romantique*—has little in common with his pupil's.

An accomplished painter and etcher, Jongkind is seen, perhaps, to better advantage in etching than in painting. His work, which is always personal, is distinguished now and then by a fine combination of breadth of treatment, vigour of sentiment, and completeness of style. On the other hand, his colour is often frigid, and his outline insistent and hard: defects the harder to forgive as his province is landscape, as he deals by preference with the broken moonlight, the misty aspects, the luminous yet hazy skies of his native country, and as he is an inheritor not of Bidault and Valenciennes, but of Constable and Isabey. It is significant, however, that most of his pictures have found a home in France, where he is greatly esteemed, though his Salon successes have been few.

131. **Moonlight on the Meuse.**
   Summer moonlight on a river, with a sloop coming down before the wind in mid-stream, and a number of trees and windmills on the right bank. 12½ by 16¼ inches. 32 by 42 *centimètres*. [991.
   Lent by ANDREW J. KIRKPATRICK, Esq., Glasgow.

132. **Landscape.**
   A river under the light of a summer moon, with boats in mid-stream, and trees and windmills on the left bank. 12¼ by 18 *inches*. 32 by 46 *centimètres*. [1056.
   Lent by D. MACDONALD, Esq., Stroove.

133. **On the Meuse.**
   A stretch of river, dotted with smacks sailing under a stiff breeze. 9¼ by 12½ inches. 23·50 by 32 *centimètres*. [1062.
   Lent by ANDREW J. KIRKPATRICK, Esq., Glasgow.

JEAN-AUGUSTE-HENRI LEYS

1814—1869

ENRI LEYS was a pupil of Ferdinand de Braekleer (1792-1883), who was a pupil of Mattheus van Brée, who was a pupil of Vincent (1746-1816) in Paris, and in 1796 was second Prix de Rome. It is natural therefore that, good colourist as he was, he should have practised historical art for the sake, not so much of passion and romance, as of correct drawing, sound painting, and careful realisation of character.

He began to exhibit as early as 1833; and as the interest of his subjects was national and patriotic, he was soon a painter of repute. His popularity only increased with years. He was made a Baron in 1862; and when he died his name and fame had become (it appeared) almost as distinguishing a feature in the history of his native city as those of Rubens himself. He was Principal of the Academy; he was chosen to decorate the Hôtel de Ville; and since his death a statue in his honour has been set up in the Park. And he was scarcely less esteemed abroad than at home. Examples of his art are to be found not only in the public collections at Brussels and at Antwerp, but in the Berlin Gallery, at Frankfort and South Kensington and Windsor Castle, at Amsterdam in the Van der Hoop Museum and in the Pinacothek at Munich; while in Paris, after gaining a Third Class medal at the Salon of 1846, and the red ribbon next year, he was awarded (for his *Trentaines de Berthall de Haze*) the Medal of Honour at the Exposition Universelle of 1855, and at that of 1867 he received a Second Class medal, and was gazetted an officer in the Legion, when, as we have seen, the loss of the latter distinction cost Rousseau his self-respect and his life.

There were two painters in Leys. In his earlier work—his studies of manners, and the aspects of things as they are—he was obviously in sympathy with modern aims, and was able to unite a fine atmospheric quality with masterly handling and genuine dignity of style. Some twelve years before his death, however, his manner changed, and he became the Belgian Pre-Raphaelite—the pupil and direct inheritor of the Van Eycks—whom Dante Rossetti esteemed to be the greatest, because the most original, master of the century, and whom others decline to regard as anything but a maker of solid and workmanlike *pastiches*—as an artist utterly lacking in the creative faculty, and producing his best work under the impulse of an inspiration partly imitative and partly one of archæology. It is said that even in Belgium, as was shown by the middling success achieved by his work at the Exposition Nationale in 1880, his vogue has had its day; that hereafter he is like to be more generously regarded for the personal quality of his few etchings than for the severe and studious unoriginality displayed in his innumerable pictures; that his best pupils resemble him least; that those who have imitated him directly have done nothing worthy of serious consideration. But, when all is said in his disfavour that can be, there remains no manner of doubt that he was a painter. His greater pictures are marked by real learning, elaborate finish, careful draughtsmanship, the most ingenious brushwork. It is true that they are deficient in the essentials of modern art: often the lines are rigid, the colour is coldly brilliant, the enveloping medium artificial and conventional. But they are master's work, though the master is not of to-day.

As a teacher Baron Leys enjoyed a great reputation, and exercised a wide and beneficent influence. Among his pupils were Messrs. Lawrence Alma Tadema, Napier Hemy, James Tissot, and Henri de Braekleer.

---

134. Antwerp during the Spanish Occupation : Christmas Day.

In the background the roofs of the city white with snow. In the foreground a snow-covered quay, with groups of men and women in sixteenth century costume. To the right a canal, with skaters and a bridge. 19 by 80½ *inches.* 48·33 *centimètres by 2 mètres 4 centimètres.* [1069.

Lent by JOHN GRAHAM, Esq., Skelmorlie Castle.

JACOBUS MARIS

BORN AT THE HAGUE, 1837

HE father of the brothers Maris was himself a painter, and his three sons, who began to draw while they were schoolboys, were all his pupils. They have, however, nothing else in common. Each is individual; none is like the others. They might have been born of different parents and at different epochs, and seemed more of a family than they do.

The eldest and strongest of the three is Jacobus, or, as we should say in English, James. When he left the Hague and his father's studio, he went to Antwerp first of all, where he studied at the Academy, and then (in 1865) to Paris, where he worked under Édouard Hébert, himself a pupil of Couture (1815-1879), and at the École des Beaux-Arts (1865-1869). At his first Salon, that of 1866, he exhibited a *Petite Fille Italienne*; at that of 1868 a *Récolte des Pommes* and a *Bords du Rhin: Hollande*; at that of 1869 a *Tricoteuse* and an *Enfant Malade*. After this, with occasional lapses into figure-painting, he appears to have devoted himself to landscape, for in the Salons of 1872, 1873, 1874 he was represented by a *Village Hollandais*, a *Canal*, and a *Vue d'Amsterdam*, while he figured at the Exposition Universelle of 1878 as the painter of a *Sur la Plage* and a *Paysage Hollandais*. He is well known in London, but has not, I believe, exhibited at Burlington House: he has been content with a place in the Goupil Gallery, to which he has sent a great deal of his best work. As he is not less facile than industrious, and paints with equal freedom in oils and water-colours, his achievement—which comprehends all manner of subjects, qualities, and sizes—is already very large.

At his highest he produces work that takes rank with the best of its time. He is not always a poet: the tone of what he does is commonly that of prose. But the prose (to carry on the metaphor) is master's work; it is stamped with a fine sincerity; in vigour and directness and variety it is not just now to be surpassed. In his pictures of man there is very little human interest. The figure is considered and handled much as though it were a piece of still life—in relation, that is, to its aërial envelope—and not for the sake of any intrinsic element of character or sentiment; so that the result is only pictorially good, and appeals to none save an æsthetic emotion. It is otherguess work with his landscape. Not only is it large in treatment, dignified in style, and finely, albeit simply, decorative in effect. You see at once that here the man's heart and brain are in entire and perfect consonance: he has felt as well as understood his subject, and the record is affecting as the experience was passionate. He is one of nature's intimates; and his expression of the peculiar sentiment of this or of that of her innumerable moods is scarce less just than his rendering of its special aspect is accurate. His skies are a case in point. None since Constable, the ancestor with whom to my mind he has most in common, has rendered clouds—the mass and the gait of them, the shadow and the light, the mystery and the wonder and the beauty—with such an insight into essentials, and such a command of appropriate and moving terms as Jacobus Maris. He paints them, not solid and still, but active in space, full of the daylight and the wind, menacing with storm, or charged with the benediction of the rain; and they look upon you from his canvasses like the living children of the weather that they are.

---

135. **The Sisters.**

Painted in water-colours. An interior, with a little blonde girl in white talking to a baby in a high chair at the tea-table. A scheme of blue, white, and black, with a red note in the carpet. 20½ *by* 17 *inches.* 52 *by* 43 *centimètres.* [1009.

Lent by JOHN S. URE, Esq., Helensburgh.

·136. **Canal with Hay-Cart.**

Painted in water-colours. A barge loading from a hay-cart at a riverside wharf, under grey clouds, through which the sun is breaking. 16 *by* 19½ *inches.* 40·50 *by* 49·50 *centimètres.* [1010.

Lent by ONE OF THE COMMITTEE.

DUTCH PICTURES

137. Distant View of Amsterdam.

A massive pile of cumulus over a still, wide river. On a low bank, running into the centre from the right, a group of scattered houses with a small wharf, at which are smacks and boats. On the foreground river, a boat with one man. 14½ by 23 inches. 37 by 58·50 centimètres. [1058.

Lent by ONE OF THE COMMITTEE.

138. Souvenir de Dordrecht.

A river crowded with barges. To the left a quay with plump and leafy trees; in the centre the cathedral; in the distance, to the right, the city; over all a tremendous mass of cloud. 40 by 56½ inches. 1 mètre 1·50 centimètres by 1 mètre 45·50 centimètres. [1060A.

Lent by ONE OF THE COMMITTEE.

139. Clouds Passing over Downs.

Painted in water-colours. A sky of moving cumuli, with a stretch of sand dunes beneath. On the horizon a church, and upon it a gleam of light accentuated by a shadow on a group of houses in the middle distance. 11¼ by 16½ inches. 28·50 by 42 centimètres. [1047.

Lent by ONE OF THE COMMITTEE.

140. **The Flageolet Player.**
A brown boy, on a red carpet, playing the flageolet from a white sheet of music, against a background of green tapestry. *13½ by 9 inches. 34·50 by 23 centimètres.*
[1033.
Lent by ONE OF THE COMMITTEE.

141. **On the Y.**
A seaport scene. A reach of water, with warehouses and ships. *8 by 14 inches. 20·33 by 35·50 centimètres.*
[1034.
Lent by JAMES STAAT-FORBES, Esq., London.

142. **The Beggar.**
A full-face and full-length study of a beggar man seated on a bench. A low-toned scheme of brown, blue, and green. *8 by 6 inches. 20·25 by 15·25 centimètres.*
[992.
Lent by JOHN A. CAMPBELL, Esq., Glasgow.

143. **Landscape with River.**
A squalid-looking village on the banks of a still river. In the background a windmill and trees, under a sky of lowering cumuli. *16½ by 24 inches. 42 by 61 centimètres.*
[1031.
Lent by ARTHUR SANDERSON, Esq., Edinburgh.

144. Moonlight.

The moon in a sky of hurrying cloud. Underneath, a marshy river with windmills. The finished sketch for the *Landscape: Moonlight* numbered 1038 in the Catalogue. 20 by 24 inches. 51 by 61 centimètres. [1054.

Lent by ONE OF THE COMMITTEE.

145. The Drawbridge.

A view up a reach of water, with masses of warehouses on the left, and in the distance a swing-bridge. 10½ by 9½ inches. 26·50 by 24 centimètres. [1022.

Lent by JAMES STAAT-FORBES, Esq., London.

146. The Drawbridge.

Painted in water-colours. The sketch, reversed, for the *Canal Bridge* numbered 986 in the *Catalogue*. 10 by 17½ inches. 25·50 by 44·50 centimètres. [1061.

Lent by ONE OF THE COMMITTEE.

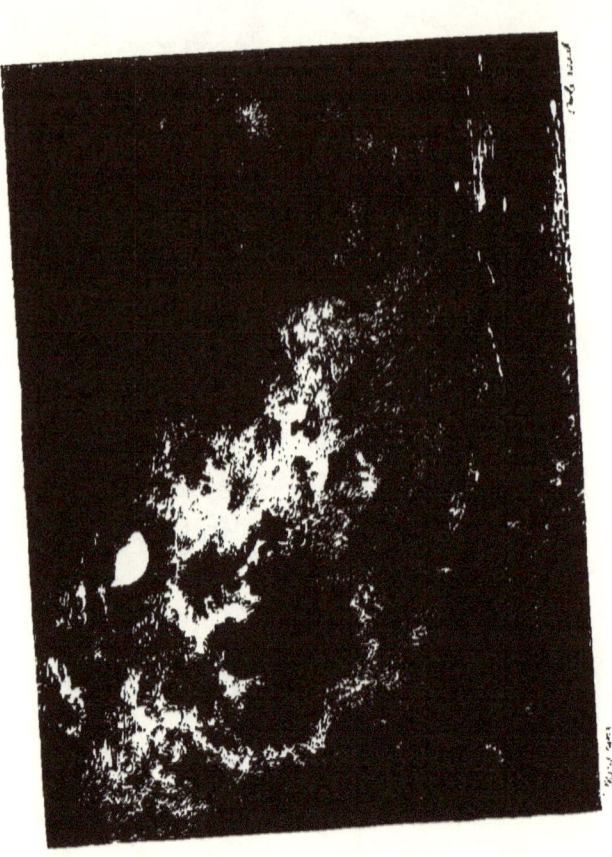

J. MARIS

147. Canal and Town : Rain Passing.

Painted in water-colours. A canal and towpath lead into the picture towards a town in the far distance, under a light rain-cloud with the sunshine glittering through it. A scheme of delicate silvery grey and green, touched with an emphatic note from certain figures on the towpath. 13¼ by 9¼ inches. 33·33 by 23·20 *centimètres*. [997.

Lent by ONE OF THE COMMITTEE.

148. Fishing-Boat at Sea.

A study of dirty weather, with smacks riding at anchor. 8½ by 11¼ inches. 21·50 by 28·50 *centimètres*. [1025.

Lent by ONE OF THE COMMITTEE.

149. Landscape : Moonlight.

The moon in a sky of hurrying and tumbled storm-clouds. Underneath, a marshy river with a boat moored to the left bank, on which are a couple of windmills. From the nearer of these a gleam of firelight. 36½ by 49½ inches. 93 *centimètres by* 1 *mètre* 25·50 *centimètres*. [1038.

ETCHING. Lent by THE HON. MR. JUSTICE DAY, London.

150. The Snow-storm.

Painted in water-colours. A stormy winter evening closing in on a cottage in the snow, which is separated by a line of stunted willows from a frozen river leading into the distance. 13½ by 15¼ *inches.* 34·33 by 39·50 *centimètres.* [1050.

Lent by JOHN A. CAMPBELL, Esq., Glasgow.

151. Souvenir de Dordrecht.

A river with a crowd of barges, and an effect of sunlight. On the left houses and trees. In the distance a town half-veiled in mist, and in the middle distance the towering mass of a cathedral. 28 by 49 *inches.* 71 *centimètres by* 1 *mètre* 24·50 *centimètres.* [1029.

ETCHING. *Lent by* THOMAS GLEN ARTHUR, Esq., Glasgow.

152. The Canal Bridge.

In the centre of the picture a bridge, under which is passing a barge laden with sand. On the left a towpath, with red-tiled houses and a woman in black with a milk-can. Under the bridge a view of the canal, with barges, and in the distance a town. 19¾ by 30 *inches.* 50 by 76 *centimètres.* [986.

Lent by ANDREW MAXWELL, Esq., Glasgow.

153. **View of a Town.**

Painted in water-colours. A view of Dordrecht. In front, a river with barges. On the left the quay, with houses and trees; the cathedral in the centre; the city in the distance to the right. The sketch for the *Souvenir de Dordrecht* numbered 1060A in the *Catalogue*. 18¼ by 25½ inches. 46·50 by 65 centimètres. [1051.

Lent by THOMAS GLEN ARTHUR, Esq., Glasgow.

154. **Landscape with Windmills.**

A flat meadow, with a canal, and on the left a windmill. A procession of enormous rain-clouds, with a single gleam of light upon the right bank of the canal and on a second windmill in the middle distance. 14¼ by 22½ inches. 35·50 by 57 centimètres. [1008.

Lent by THE HON. MR. JUSTICE DAY, London.

155. **The Towing-Path.**

Painted in water-colours. An evening effect. On a towpath leading into the picture two horses with their riders, in relief against a sandy distance and the sky beyond. 11¼ by 7 inches. 28·50 by 17·75 centimètres. [1001.

Lent by ONE OF THE COMMITTEE.

MATTHŸS MARIS

BORN AT THE HAGUE, 1839

HE life of Matthew Maris has been altogether secluded and uneventful. There is no more to tell of him than that he began, like his brother James, at the Antwerp Academy; that in 1867 he went to Paris, where he studied under Hébert and at the École des Beaux-Arts; that he came to London ten years after, and has made his home there ever since; that he is averse from publicity and contemptuous of distinction, and is content to paint for himself and his few friends.

He is an artist of rare parts and singular accomplishment. He mastered his craft almost at starting; and his earliest work is distinguished by sanity of aim and completeness of method. But it is not in his earliest work that he can be rightly savoured. He has in him a vein of poetry, a strain of imagination, that is none the less intense for being somewhat morbid and unsound; and he was quick to part company with solid earth, and to become a painter of dreams. He is not concerned with the outward show of things, but with their spiritual shapes, their attribute of mystery, their inner essence and innate significance; and he expresses as much of these as is revealed to him in terms of strange and peculiar beauty. His view of life is melancholy; his sympathies are curiously individual and remote; his humanity is warped, fantastic, even elf-like; his romance, for all the close and brooding passion with which it is expressed, is so uncommon as to appear unreal. But he has a magic of his own, and to withstand his incantations is impossible. Their appeal is vague as that in certain of Heine's verses—

> Aus alten Märchen winkt es
> Hervor mit weisser Hand,
> Da singt es und da klingt es
> Von einem Zauberland—

and withal as curiously affecting. I do not want to strain the comparison. Heine is the most human of poets; Matthew Maris is one of the least sexual of painters. But I confess that to me the Dutchman's pictures are now and then inevitably suggestive of the more fantastic and far-away of the greater artist's lyrics. They might almost pass for illustrations of certain pages in the *Buch der Lieder*, just as certain pages in the *Buch der Lieder* recall to me with no uncertain voice the unearthly glamour, "the light that never was on sea or land," which shimmers from so much of the painter's work. Here is an instance of what I mean:—

> Im Zaubergarten wallen
> Zwei Buhlen stumm und allein,
> Es singen die Nachtigallen,
> Es flimmert der Mondenschein.

That, with what follows, is a Matthew Maris in words.

His art—though Israels has described it as "the fine gold of Dutch painting"—will always be caviare to the general. It may be, indeed, that the half of him will not be told to us; for his life is spent in the pursuit of unattainable perfections, and he regards the most of those pictures which he consents to part with as no more than experiments or failures. It may, however, be said of these, that, whatever their author's opinion of them, they are good enough for them that have eyes to see. If they proved no more, they would still prove that two great and precious qualities are indisputably his. He has a gift of exquisite colour and an infallible sense of tone. Of late the former potency has suffered change: his reveries have grown sombre and sad; he has done with his weird yet lovely combinations of magical blue and ethereal gold; he paints not dreams, but the melancholy ghosts of dreams. But his tonality is always faultless; and those, perhaps, who have caught the full perfume of his subtle and peculiar genius will find new charm in his darkening mood.

156. A Head.

A powerfully painted study, dark almost to blackness, of a female head and face. 11¾ by 9 inches. 30 by 22·75 centimètres. [1023.

Lent by E. J. VAN WISSELINGH, Esq., The Hague.

157. Figure of a Girl.

A girl (half-length) in a kitchen. An arrangement of delicate brown, pink, and white. 12½ by 8 inches. 32 by 20·25 centimètres. [989.

Lent by DANIEL COTTIER, Esq., London.

158. Figure: Evening.

Drawn in charcoal. A woman at work with her spindle and distaff. 11⅜ by 7⅝ inches. 29 by 19·25 centimètres. [994A.

Lent by ONE OF THE COMMITTEE.

159. A Child's Head.

Portrait-study of a baby's head. 9¼ by 7¾ inches. 23·50 by 19·75 centimètres. [996.

Lent by E. J. VAN WISSELINGH, Esq., The Hague.

160. The Castle.

A fantasy in silver-grey. A magic wood, with a ghostly castle in the background. 8 by 13 inches. 20·33 by 33 centimètres. [1012.

Lent by E. J. VAN WISSELINGH, Esq., The Hague.

161. Still-Life.

Study of a powder-horn and belt, painted literally and with the utmost minuteness of finish. 16 by 12½ inches. 40·50 by 32 centimètres. [1004.

Lent by E. J. VAN WISSELINGH, Esq., The Hague.

DUTCH PICTURES

162. Landscape.

A foreground of ploughed field with a cottage, behind which a meadow with dwarf trees slopes down to a lake that is touched with light from a warm, white evening sky. 7½ by 10¼ inches. 19 by 26 centimètres. [1013.

Lent by E. J. VAN WISSELINGH, Esq., The Hague.

163. Le Ménage.

A woman washing clothes in a cottage back-garden. In the background trees, cottages, and a church relieved against an evening sky. A scheme of dark green and grey. 15 by 10½ inches. 38 by 26·75 centimètres. [1016.

ETCHING. *Lent by* JAMES STAAT-FORBES, Esq., London.

164. Landscape with Goats.

A sandy bank topped with scrubby bushes. On the left a dusky gully. In the distance, dimly seen through a silvery mist, a castle. A white goat and her kid in the foreground, with a young, stunted oak-tree to the right. 14 by 17½ inches. 35·50 by 44·20 centimètres. [1006.

Lent by ONE OF THE COMMITTEE.

165. **Going to School.**

A mother starting her little one to school. Under a verandah, in rear of the two principal figures, a baby on a bench. An effect of dazzling morning sunshine flickering through leaves. 4 by 6¾ inches. 10 by 17 centimètres. [994.

Lent by JAMES STAAT-FORBES, Esq., London.

166, 167, 168, 169. **Dancing.**

Four decorative panels in dead oil colour. On each a dancing girl, half-nude and lightly draped in grey gauze, is shown in relief against a tracery of bronze-coloured leaves on a black ground. 57½ by 22¼ inches. 1 mètre 46 centimètres by 56·50 centimètres. [1026, 1027, 1036, 1037.

Lent by ONE OF THE COMMITTEE.

170. Souvenir d'Amsterdam.

    A sea-port scene. In the foreground a barge passing under a balance-bridge. To the right a small black figure. A delicate arrangement in white and reddish grey. 17½ by 13¼ inches. 44·50 by 33·50 centimètres. [1017.

Lent by DANIEL COTTIER, Esq., London.

171. Landscape with Squirrels.

    An autumn-tinted wood, with a castle seen vaguely through the trees. In the centre two tiny mediæval lovers, and in the foreground a red squirrel. 11½ by 18 inches. 29 by 46 centimètres. [1048.

Lent by ONE OF THE COMMITTEE.

172. The Spinner.

    Drawn in charcoal. A night effect, with a woman, holding a distaff, prostrate on the floor of (apparently) a small room. 19 by 26¼ inches. 48·33 by 66·50 centimètres. [1028.

Lent by ONE OF THE COMMITTEE.

173. Girl with Goats.

    A girl in yellow with a distaff seated against a bank. Among scrub to the left a white goat and kid. In the distance a magic castle. 25 by 38½ inches. 63·50 by 98 centimètres. [1059.

Lent by ROBERT RAMSEY, Esq., Glasgow.

174. Tending Ducks.

    A girl sitting on a rail and watching a brood of ducks. A scheme of delicate half-tones, in which the one emphatic note is the heroine's red cap. 13¼ by 9 inches. 33·33 by 23 centimètres. [1032.

Lent by ALEXANDER BOWMAN, Esq., Glasgow.

175. Portrait of The Painter.

Study of the face alone against a background of plain red. 10¼ by 7 inches. 26·50 by 17·75 centimètres. [1035.

Lent by JAMES MARIS, Esq., The Hague.

176. "He is Coming!"

A rich interior, with cabinets and bric-à-brac, in which a girl with flowing red hair, in a mediæval costume of grey and yellow, is seated, listening, at a distaff. In the doorway a young man with a cross-bow. 17 by 12¾ inches. 43 by 32·50 centimètres. [1044.

ETCHING. *Lent by* ONE OF THE COMMITTEE.

177. The Sisters.

An impression of a girl leaning on a grassy sand-bank, with a child clinging about her neck. A scheme of pale, greenish grey, with faint notes of red and pale black. 39 by 25 inches. 99 by 63·50 centimètres. [1052.

Lent by PERCY WESTMACOTT, Esq., Newcastle-on-Tyne.

WILLEM MARIS

BORN AT THE HAGUE, 1844

ALLED "de Zilveren," or "the Silvery," the youngest of the Maris brothers has no particular history. Like his elders, Jacobus and Matthÿs, he began to draw while he was yet a schoolboy, and was to some extent a pupil of his father. Unlike them, however, he did not go abroad in search of instruction, but stayed and learned his art at home.

Like Troyon, he is a painter of cattle and the country. His range is narrow, but he has a place and a function of his own. He delights in the study and the presentation of delicate haze and warm sunshine, the play of light upon quiet streams and brilliant foliage, the varied tones of green in grassy distances, the grouping and the sentiment of drinking and loitering herds, or herds at rest in the mid-day heat. He is never the most vigorous of painters; but his work is seldom lacking in distinction, and has often a peculiar charm.

---

178. A Cow.

 A white cow in a stable, facing outward from the picture. 7½ by 9¼ inches. 19 by 23·50 centimètres. [993.

       Lent by DANIEL COTTIER, Esq., London.

179. Landscape with Cattle.

 Cows grazing in a stretch of sunlit pasture sloping from the right down to a small stream, on the left of which are tall trees. 10¾ by 8 inches. 27·50 by 20·33 centimètres. [1065.

       Lent by THE HON. MR. JUSTICE DAY, London.

180. Landscape : Cow Drinking.

A stretch of sunlit pasture with a pool in the foreground, at which is drinking a black and white cow.   8 by 11 *inches.*   20·33 by 28 *centimètres.*   [1043.

Lent by JAMES STAAT-FORBES, Esq., London.

181. Cows in Meadow.

A sunlit meadow, with cattle wading in a willow-fringed brook. A brilliantly clear effect of light and heat.   22½ by 43½ *inches.*   57 *centimètres by* 1 *mètre* 10·50 *centimètres.*   [1046.

Lent by JAMES MYLNE, Esq., Edinburgh.

ANTON MAUVE

BORN at ZAANDAM, 1838

AUVE is a pupil of Pieter Frederik Van Os (born 1808). His official successes have been neither few nor unimportant. He is represented in the Ryksmuseum, at Rotterdam, and at the Hague; he is a member of the Dutch Society of Arts and Sciences and the Société des Aquarellistes Belges, and a Knight of the Order of Leopold; and he has been the recipient of medals at Philadelphia, Amsterdam, Vienna, Antwerp, and Paris.

He is not to be ranked with Troyon. He is much less vigorous and less original; he is not nearly so great a painter; his work is not so solid in execution or so decorative in effect. But among living artists he is very far from being the least. His draughtsmanship is sound, his brushwork full of gusto and expression, his colour quite his own; to a right sense of nature and a mastery of certain atmospheric effects he unites a genuine strain of poetry. In pure landscape he is often excellent: he paints it with a brilliant combination of knowledge and feeling. His treatment of animals is at once judicious and affectionate. He is careful to render them in relation to their aërial surroundings; but he has recognised that they too are creatures of character and sentiment, and he loves to paint them in their relations to each other and to man. The sentiment is never forced, the characterisation is never strained, the drama is never exorbitant; the proportions in which they are introduced are so nicely adjusted that the pictorial, the purely artistic, quality of the work is undiminished. To Troyon animals were objects in a landscape; to Mauve they are that and something more. His old horses are their old masters' friends; his cows are used to the girls who tend them; his sheep feed as though they knew each other and liked it. In a word, his use of the dramatic element is primarily artistic; and it is with something of a blush that one compares his *savoir-vivre* with the bad manners of some animal painters nearer home.

He is still in his prime, and (it may be opined) has not yet spoken his last word. It may further be noted that he paints in water-colours with so ready a brush that, as often as not, he has no time to do himself justice.

---

182. A Horse.

A white horse in a stable, his tail towards the door. 6¾ by 9¼ *inches.* 17·33 by 23·50 *centimètres.* [990.

Lent by DANIEL COTTIER, Esq., London.

183. An Ox.

A white-floored stable, with a red and white ox lying among reeds, against a background of grey boarding. 17 by 26¼ *inches.* 43 by 67·33 *centimètres.* [1068.

Lent by ONE OF THE COMMITTEE.

184. Cattle in Meadow.

Under a sky of greenish-blue, in a meadow of greyish-green, a woman tending three cows, one red and white, the other white and black. 19¼ by 39½ inches. 49 centimètres by 1 mètre. [1018.

Lent by THE HON. MR. JUSTICE DAY, London.

185. Girl Leading Cow.

A girl in sabots and a blue apron leading two cows to pasture. A background of grey palings and small trees. To the right, an outlook upon dunes. 21½ by 39½ inches. 54·50 centimètres by 1 mètre. [1040.

ETCHING. *Lent by* ONE OF THE COMMITTEE.

186. The Sand-Cart.

Two horses yoked tandem to a laden cart and relieved against a brilliantly-lighted beach, with grey sea and pale blue sky. 21½ by 39½ inches. 54·50 centimètres by 1 mètre. [1060.

Lent by JAMES MYLNE, Esq., Edinburgh.

187. Marshes : Evening.

A flat and wide expanse of grey marshland under a sky of rolling grey cloud. 22¾ by 35 inches. 58 by 89 centimètres. [1000.

Lent by THE HON. MR. JUSTICE DAY, London.

HENDRIK WILLEM MESDAG

BORN AT GRONINGEN, 1831

BORN a rich man, Mesdag did not begin to paint in earnest till he was five-and-thirty years old. Then he worked at Brussels under Roelof, and had lessons from Alma Tadema. His rise was rapid and steady. He was medalled at the Salon of 1870; eight years after, he received a Third Class distinction at the Exposition Universelle; in 1880 he won a Gold medal at the Hague; at the Salon of 1887 he attained to First Class honours with an admirable *Soleil Couchant*; he has been this some time past an officer of the Order of Leopold; so that he cannot be said to have gone without reward.

It is right to add that the reward is well deserved. Mesdag has not only intelligence and strength of will, but a fine temperament also. He started late, but one would never know it from his work, which is distinguished by the possession of solid merits of sentiment and observation, and by excellent accomplishment as well. His province is the sea; and by his rendering of some among its many moods and aspects he has made himself an honourable place among good modern painters.

---

188. The Sea : Sunset.

A long, low reach of grey sand, with the sea beyond, and over all a quiet sunset sky. 16½ by 39¼ *inches.* 42 by 100 *centimètres.* [988.

Lent by THE HON. MR. JUSTICE DAY, London.

130   DUTCH PICTURES

189. Dutch Fishing-Boats.

Two fishing-boats riding at anchor in-shore in a gale of wind. 23 by 18½ inches.
58·50 by 47 centimètres. [1049.

Lent by D. M. MACDONALD, Esq., Glasgow.

ALBERT NEUHUYS

Born at Utrecht, 1844

NEUHUYS received his first lessons from a local master, Gisbert de Craayvanger (born 1810); was four years a student in the Antwerp Academy; was medalled at Amsterdam in 1872, and again in 1880 at Paris, for contributions to the Exhibition of Works in Black and White. I shall have told all I know when I have noted that he is popular in England and America, and that a picture of his is hung in the Rÿksmuseum, Amsterdam.

He follows the lead of Israels, but with a lighter and brighter humour, and often with a greater and showier power of composition. He is a sound craftsman, and his colour, though it lacks distinction, is good of its kind. His chief fault is that he paints for the public. The Dutch baby is (no doubt) an interesting creature; but it is easy to have too much of him, and the greater the skill with which he is treated, the less desirable after a certain course of him does his company appear. That at least is the conclusion imposed upon one by the work of Albert Neuhuys.

---

190. **An Interesting Story.**

An interior, in which a young woman, seated at a round table, is teaching a little girl to read. A scheme of grey-blue and black, with suggestions of red on the woman's cap, the table, and the floor. 26¾ by 19¼ *inches.* 68 *by* 50 *centimètres.*
[1045.

Lent by JOHN G. URE, Esq., Helensburgh.

191. Hide-and-Seek.

A cottage interior, with the housewife at her needle, and her children playing bo-peep about her knees. 19½ by 15¾ inches. 49·50 by 40·25 centimètres.

[1005.

Lent by MRS. DUBS, Glasgow.

FREDERIK PIETER TER MEULEN

Born at Bodegraven (South Holland), 1843

CATTLE-painting was Ter Meulen's study in early youth, under Hendrik Van de Sande Backhuizen (1795-1860). He was presently constrained, however, to abandon painting for other work; and it was only after the lapse of full ten years—during which time he studied at the University of Leyden—that he was able to return to it. Since this second start he has prospered and become popular, though he has never gained a distinction. He has written, too, about the theory of art; and as his work is greatly esteemed by his fellow-craftsmen, it can hardly be other than intelligent and sound.

His painting is technically sound, its quality is good, it is taking in effect. Its chief characteristic is unoriginality: it suggests for the most part not Ter Meulen, but Mauve or Willem Maris. Much of the best of it is in water-colours, in whose use the artist is uncommonly facile and adroit; but both in water-colours and in oils it has, with the merit of being always pleasant, the fault of being never great. The reproach is fatal to its chances with the future, but has the opposite effect upon its position in the present.

---

192. Cows in Meadow.

A group of cattle pasturing in bright sunlight, under a pale blue sky. 13¼ by 25½ inches. 33·75 by 65·25 centimètres. [987.

Lent by JOHN WORDIE, Esq., Glasgow.

www.ingramcontent.com/pod-product-compliance
Lightning Source LLC
Chambersburg PA
CBHW021819230426
43669CB00008B/804